The next time I'm including a copy of *Motherhood Is Not Your Highest Calling*. As an empty nester with grown children who are now parents themselves, Vicki brings wise, needed, and loving perspective to the gifts and challenges of motherhood (which, unfortunately, can sometimes feel like an all-consuming competitive sport). Vicki lovingly and graciously questions some of the messages we've internalized about what a mother's life "should" look like, and as she does that, she encourages women to lay down unrealistic expectations and parent from a place of grace and freedom. What a relief to remember that an abundant life has lots of different parts—and while motherhood is undoubtedly a meaningful one, it's not the *only* one.

SOPHIE HUDSON, bestselling author of *A Fine Sight to See* and cohost of *The Big Boo Cast*

Motherhood Is Not Your Highest Calling: The Grace of Being a Good-Enough Mom will help set you free from the unrealistic standards placed on mothers. Vicki not only unpacks the lies we believe (which cause endless guilt, shame, and condemnation) but offers a way forward leading to the abundant life Jesus has for every mother. Do yourself a favor and read this if you're even contemplating having children one day.

CHRISTINE CAINE, founder of A21 and Propel Women

This book is a lifeline for every mom drowning in guilt, comparison, or busyness. You don't have to be everything. You just have to belong to the one who is.

    DANNAH GRESH, founder of True Girl and bestselling author of *Lies Girls Believe: And the Truth That Sets Them Free*

My only issue with this book is that I didn't have it eighteen years ago as a new mom. No matter your season of motherhood, we all need the freedom to put motherhood in its proper place to free our hearts from an unattainable pursuit. Another must-read by Vicki!

    COURTNEY DEFEO, speaker, blogger, and author of *In This House, We Will Giggle*

This book felt like a deep breath I didn't know I was holding. With humility and hard-won wisdom, Vicki Courtney speaks straight to the ache of moms who've been told their worth is tied to how well they parent. She dismantles the myth of motherhood as our highest calling and points us back to the gentle, grace-filled way of Jesus. *Motherhood Is Not Your Highest Calling* is the kind of truth telling that sets women free.

    CASSANDRA SPEER, bestselling author, Bible teacher, podcast host, and vice president of Her True Worth

MOTHERHOOD IS NOT YOUR HIGHEST CALLING

The Grace of Being a Good-Enough Mom

VICKI COURTNEY

NavPress
Published in alliance with Tyndale House Publishers

NavPress
Bold. Loving. Sensible.

NavPress.com

Motherhood Is Not Your Highest Calling: The Grace of Being a Good-Enough Mom

Copyright © 2025 by Vicki Courtney. All rights reserved.

A NavPress resource published in alliance with Tyndale House Publishers

NavPress is a registered trademark of NavPress, The Navigators, Colorado Springs, CO. The NavPress logo is a trademark of NavPress, The Navigators, Colorado Springs, CO. *Tyndale* is a registered trademark of Tyndale House Ministries. Absence of ® in connection with marks of NavPress or other parties does not indicate an absence of registration of those marks.

The Team:
David Zimmerman, Publisher; Caitlyn Carlson, Senior Editor; Elizabeth Schroll, Copyeditor; Lacie Phillips, Production Assistant; Sarah Ocenasek, Proofreading Coordinator

The appendix, adapted from Brittany Yesudasan's "Your Identity in Christ: How God Sees You," is used with permission from the copyright holder.

Cover design by Faceout Studio, Molly von Borstel.

Cover and interior images licensed under subscription plan from Shutterstock.com. All rights reserved.

Author photo copyright © 2024 by Jenny Petty Photography. All rights reserved.

All Scripture quotations, unless otherwise indicated, are taken from the Holy Bible, *New International Version*,® *NIV*.® Copyright © 1973, 1978, 1984, 2011 by Biblica, Inc.® Used by permission. All rights reserved worldwide. Scripture quotations marked CSB are taken from the Christian Standard Bible,® copyright © 2017 by Holman Bible Publishers. Used by permission. Christian Standard Bible® and CSB® are federally registered trademarks of Holman Bible Publishers. Scripture quotations marked ESV are from The ESV® Bible (The Holy Bible, English Standard Version®), copyright © 2001 by Crossway, a publishing ministry of Good News Publishers. Used by permission. All rights reserved. Scripture quotation marked KJV is taken from the *Holy Bible*, King James Version. Scripture quotations marked MSG are taken from *The Message*, copyright © 1993, 2002, 2018 by Eugene H. Peterson. Used by permission of NavPress. All rights reserved. Represented by Tyndale House Publishers. Scripture quotations marked NLT are taken from the *Holy Bible*, New Living Translation, copyright © 1996, 2004, 2015 by Tyndale House Foundation. Used by permission of Tyndale House Publishers, Carol Stream, Illinois 60188. All rights reserved.

Published in association with literary agent Don Gates of the Gates Group, the-gates-group.com

Some of the anecdotal illustrations in this book are true to life and are included with the permission of the persons involved. All other illustrations are composites of real situations, and any resemblance to people living or dead is purely coincidental.

For information about special discounts for bulk purchases, please contact Tyndale House Publishers at csresponse@tyndale.com, or call 1-855-277-9400.

ISBN 978-1-64158-871-3

Printed in the United States of America

31 30 29 28 27 26 25
7   6   5   4   3   2   1

CONTENTS

INTRODUCTION Too Much and Never Enough **1**

ONE More Than a Mom
The Grace of Remembering Who You Are **11**

TWO Cancel the Guilt Trip
The Grace of Being Imperfect **37**

THREE Good for Her, Not for Me
The Grace of Acceptance **63**

FOUR Slow Down and Show Up
The Grace of Being Present **81**

FIVE Worry Doesn't Get to Run the Show
The Grace of Releasing What If . . . ? **101**

SIX Less Stuff, More Magic
The Grace of Simplicity **119**

SEVEN You Matter Too
The Grace of Being Kind to Yourself **137**

EPILOGUE More Than Enough **156**

APPENDIX What the Bible Says about Identity in Christ **158**

Acknowledgments **163**

Notes **165**

To my daughter, Paige, and my daughters-in-love, Casey and Becca: May you always rest in God's abundant grace of good enough.

INTRODUCTION

TOO MUCH AND NEVER ENOUGH

I was scrolling on Instagram when a video from a mom influencer popped up on my feed. Within thirty seconds, I was catapulted into the woman's homesteading life on a farm with her seven children, the youngest of whom she had recently delivered in her bathtub. Her weekend recap moved at a breakneck pace. Children circled around a table eating German pancakes with fresh whipped cream and syrup on top, all of which had been made from scratch. (And I'm not talking about pancake mix in a box or heavy whipping cream in a carton—this mom has her own milk cows and mills her own flour.) Next up was a pic of the salad of microgreens she'd grown in trays in her kitchen with a side of fresh bread made from one of many jars of sourdough starter. At the end of the video, the whole family skipped out the door for church, all dressed up and smiling.

I am more than a dozen years post–empty nest . . . and that video left me feeling like I needed to call my adult children and apologize for buying bagged salads and feeding them a steady diet of Pop-Tarts and Toaster Strudels for breakfast. The modern-day "trad wife" influencer may have been a stranger to me, but the message she was peddling was all too familiar: *Being a mom is your most important role, and getting it right with your kids is your most important job.*

Long before *trad wife* was a social-media catchphrase, I went through my own phase of experimenting with cloth diapers, making my baby food from scratch, and playing classical music in the background to enrich my children's lives. My idealistic intentions were always short-lived, smothered by the realities of motherhood, but the guilt lingered.

At some level, we're all trying to live up to some idealized version of motherhood. Some women have the resources and support to make the pursuit look seamless and tidy, but we all feel the same sense of failure when we don't measure up to the expectations mothers are bombarded with from every direction we turn. We live with a perpetual ache in our souls that we're not doing enough for our kids, that our homes are not tidy enough, our choices are not good enough, our children are not well-behaved enough—and try as we may to hit the mark, nothing we do ever seems to be enough.

Motherhood is hard, but you know that already. (For the record, I'm impressed you have the bandwidth to add this book to your plate.) But as someone down the road—my husband and I have three children who have grown up, gotten married, and blessed us with ten grandchildren—I'm here to tell you that all these weights and expectations are built on a dangerous lie. And that lie is crushing the life out of you.

You are more than a mom. No doubt your children can bring much joy to your life, but they were never intended to *become* your life. Motherhood is not your highest calling.

EXCEEDING OUR LIMIT

I see you. I see what you're carrying. You're having to manage your anxieties in the face of around-the-clock doom-and-gloom news stories about childhood dangers, societal violence, and natural disasters that can leave you wanting to Bubble Wrap your children and never leave home. You face the pressures of judgmental eyes on social media and in the grocery store and are inundated with strong opinions from armchair experts. And the nonstop discourse about gentle parenting, birth plans, health choices, and education decisions that pit mom against mom leave you questioning your own instincts and feeling like a failure.

I recently stumbled upon the term *Depleted Mother Syndrome*, which perfectly describes what many mothers are feeling. "Depleted Mother Syndrome (DMS) occurs when a mother feels emotionally, mentally, and physically drained from the constant demands of parenting."[1] In a nutshell, it's a fancy label for motherhood burnout. It's a simple equation: We are doing too much and are told we should do more—and eventually our load exceeds our limit.

I'm reminded of a recent trip where I found myself waiting for an elevator on an upper level of an airport parking garage. Out of three elevators, only one was operational, and it was taking a while for it to get to the top of the parking garage. By the time the doors opened, a crowd of people had gathered. Not wanting to miss our flights, we all crammed in until my claustrophobic self was on the verge of a panic attack. Just as the doors began to close, someone else raced up and asked, "Room for one more?" A guy toward the front yelled, "Sorry, man, we're at the maximum load limit!"

Maximum load limit is a construction term for the maximum load a structure can sustain before risking collapse. It's probably something we should pay more attention to, but most of us look right past the signs. The same is true for the load we carry as mothers. Rarely do we pay attention to the signs that we've pushed past our limits. We've accepted it as the norm and then wonder why we are often on the verge of collapsing. It's a miserable way to live, but it's all we know.

Why does this happen, and why does it feel inevitable?

Somewhere along the way we swapped *good enough* for *perfect*. Because our culture, our family systems, and our church contexts tell us that our children, our marriages, and our families depend on us not getting a single thing wrong. And, it turns out, there are just way too many things to get right.

Try harder. Do more. Get your act together. Be like her. Lose weight. Exercise. Eat better. Deal with that messy house. Play with the kids. Do the flash-card drills. Volunteer at the school. Go to church. Join a Bible study. Be a better wife. Be a better mother.

The constant pressures to live up to an unattainable standard are easier to notice in the myriad of symptoms they produce. The loss of the person you were before you had children. Running yourself ragged attempting to offer your children the best of everything, all while experiencing a nagging feeling that you're not truly present for the moments that matter most. The constant comparison to other mothers and the belief that others are doing a much better job. The clutter from overconsumption in the quest to provide all the things that contribute to a magical childhood, and the resulting angst when the magic doesn't show up as promised. The never-ending guilt trip to get everything—and I do mean *everything*—right. The undercurrent of worry over the *what-ifs* you can't stop thinking about and the constant exposure to *what-ifs* you hadn't thought about before. The neglect of your own needs and self-care in the pressure to live up to the expectation that everyone else should matter before you do.

Can you relate?

Add to all that the reality that our culture isn't set up to support moms. The contribution of stay-at-home moms is undervalued and taken for granted as moms find themselves in the endless cycle of caring for everyone else twenty-four seven while their own needs go unattended. Working moms carry the weight of helping support their families financially, balancing job demands with the stress of finding affordable childcare and managing school pickups—and feeling the guilt of being constantly torn between both worlds. All the while, moms can feel lonely and disconnected, struggling to find supportive friendships and wishing they lived closer to family who could help—or that they had family they trusted to help.

And while church should be a safe place for mothers to gather and find support, it can quickly become another place where the expectations are too much and the help is too little. A recent Barna study found that while Christian mothers are often responsible for the discipleship and faith formation of their children, they are "notably underserved" in the church.[2] "Just one in 10 U.S. pastors strongly agrees their church prioritizes mothers," the study explains, "and nearly half of moms say that their church 'never' provides materials to help support them as a mother."[3]

Mothers are in desperate need of support that extends far beyond childcare during worship services. Motherhood can be soul crushing at times, and church should be a place where mothers can come—with no strings attached—to catch their breath and be reminded that their well-being matters too. I am a huge proponent of local expressions that support the gathering together of the body of believers, and not every church is missing the mark when it comes to offering support for mothers—but many are. It's no wonder many churches are struggling to attract younger families. Show me a church where mothers feel supported, and I'll show you a growing congregation.

It doesn't take a mathematician to recognize the gross imbalance that results from an increase in expectations and a decrease in support. Something has to give. Just recently, the former surgeon general issued an advisory on the mental health and well-being of parents, highlighting the urgent need to better support them. Additionally, he called for "a fundamental shift in how we value and prioritize parents' well-being."[4] This is not all in your head. You are not alone.

You might believe that the constant white noise of *never enough* comes with the territory of motherhood. It has become your default rhythm. It's hard to even imagine a version of motherhood where you wake up free from the grip it has on your life.

But I have good news for you: You can, in fact, be free.

LIVING LIGHTLY

In Matthew 11:28-30, Jesus offers an invitation:

> "Come to me, all you who are weary and burdened, and I will give you rest. Take my yoke upon you and learn from me, for I am gentle and humble in heart, and you will find rest for your souls. For my yoke is easy and my burden is light."

The Greek word translated "burdened" in this passage is *phortizō*, which means "to load up (properly, as a vessel or animal)."[5] If you've had babies or toddlers, you've probably felt like a pack mule from time to time, carrying as many things as possible, including your child. Or as you parent older children, the emotional burdens and weighty situations may feel too heavy to bear. Both are the kind of heaviness Jesus is talking about.

But then he goes on to say, "Take my yoke upon you." A yoke is "a bar or frame of wood by which two draft animals are joined at the head or neck in order to work together effectively in pulling a plow, harrow, or wagon."[6] For years, whenever I read this passage, I assumed it was a picture of Jesus taking on our burdens. But Jesus is not saying he will carry our entire load. Nor is he saying he will adapt to *our* load capacity. He's not offering to step in and help you check all the boxes on your long to-do list. He won't help you fold the laundry, shuttle the kids to their after-school activities, or start a pot of chili on the stovetop for dinner. He doesn't wash windows, and he won't change diapers. No—Jesus offers something better: partnership rooted in the reality of who we are in him.

He wants to take you under his wing and show you a better way. He makes it clear: "*My yoke* is easy and *my burden* is light" (emphasis added). He's saying to us, "Learn from me—follow *my* lead, and trade your load for mine." The load we're carrying to be the *best mom* who never lets her kids down is the equivalent of us dragging a wagon by ourselves. Allowing Jesus to trade our load for his means that we need to take a serious look at where we've been placing our identity—and more importantly, what having this misplaced identity has done to our souls.

I won't promise you that unpacking your load will be easy (it won't), but I can promise you that it will be worth it in the end. A new perspective, new patterns, and new habits will take some time to adjust to. You didn't arrive at where you are overnight, so extend grace to yourself on the journey to gain God's perspective of who you are. The first step is to say yes to Jesus.

I love *The Message* translation of Jesus' invitation in Matthew 11:

"Are you tired? Worn out? Burned out on religion? Come to me. Get away with me and you'll recover your life. I'll show you how to take a real rest. Walk with me and work with me—watch how I do it.

Learn the unforced rhythms of grace. I won't lay anything heavy or ill-fitting on you. Keep company with me and you'll learn to live freely and lightly."

MATTHEW 11:28-30, MSG

Jesus has extended an invitation to help you *recover your life*. Do you want to take him up on his offer to "live freely and lightly"? You don't have to carry your burdens alone. The same Savior who carried the burden of his own cross to his crucifixion knows a thing or two about heavy loads. Will you let him show you the way?

ONE

MORE THAN A MOM

The Grace of Remembering Who You Are

> Remember always that you not only have the right to be an individual, you have an obligation to be one.
> **ELEANOR ROOSEVELT**

I plucked a well-worn Christian parenting book off my bookshelf one afternoon and, out of curiosity, began flipping through it. It didn't take long before my eyes landed on a phrase common in many Christian parenting books from my young-motherhood days. This particular book referenced motherhood as "a high calling" and went on to declare it "perhaps, the highest calling God can give a woman."[1] I grumbled under my breath, triggered at the false, impossibly heavy expectation that had been placed on mothers of my generation.

Sadly, the book I'd picked up was a book I had written years ago! I was part of the problem. At the time, I had sincerely believed that motherhood was a woman's highest calling, echoing what I had been taught over the years under the guise of biblical womanhood. *Biblical womanhood* had become a catchall term of directives and expectations—many of which were nowhere to be found in Scripture—that determined whether a Christian woman was sufficiently living up to who she was "meant to be." Culture at-large reinforced the expectation that a woman's life was incomplete without marriage and children. As a result, many Christian books and Bible studies reiterated this idea that marriage and motherhood were core to a woman's identity.

One Sunday years ago at my previous church, the service specifically addressed the topics of biblical womanhood and biblical manhood. The men and the women were placed in separate groups and taught a lesson that had been prepared by a male pastor on staff. I was out of town on that Sunday, but in the aftermath, multiple women reached out to me because they had found the lesson troubling.

One of the women sent me the outline, and upon reading it, I could certainly understand the concern. The lesson stated that a woman's ultimate life purpose was to "help men's worthy leadership with submission and respect and prioritize the nurturing and raising of children."

A woman in the class lodged a formal complaint to the staff that the teaching had suggested that a woman's value was directly dependent on her role as a wife and mother. She argued, "I am complete in my relationship with God, with or without a man or children." She went on to share that she had served for many years as a missionary prior to meeting her husband and that, once married, she had struggled to have children. She and her husband were in the process of adopting a child, and the lesson left her feeling as though she was "less than" or out of God's favor.

Other women took offense that the responsibility of nurturing and raising children was laid solely on their shoulders. Many worked full-time jobs to help pay the bills, some even outearning their husbands or working longer hours than them to make ends meet.

Worst of all was the fact that this brand of womanhood was (and often still is) presented as biblical, suggesting that women who don't follow the template and fulfill their so-called purpose (marrying and having children) are disobedient and outside God's will for their lives.

I thought about how hurtful this teaching is to so many women in the family of God. Single women who dream of marriage and motherhood but aren't sure that dream will ever become reality. Or married women who long to be mothers but struggle with infertility. Or women who simply don't feel called to have children. How invisible they must have all felt in a church culture telling them that marriage was what every woman was destined for and that children were a mandatory by-product of marriage. I felt a wave of compassion for all the women who had been exposed to this toxic teaching and were left wondering if they were less loved by God and all the women who were questioned and challenged over the years about being single or childless or working outside the home. This hardly sounds biblical.

That lesson became a turning point for me. I began to rethink many of the "biblical womanhood" teachings I had accepted without question over the years and sadly even recycled into some of my early books and Bible studies. Fortunately, those books are now out of print, but it grieves my heart all the same to know I may have added to the confusion and pain many Christian women experience in unpacking their identity.

I began to dig deeper into the Scriptures about the roles of women in the church and home and could find nothing that supported the assertion that a woman's primary purpose is linked to marriage and motherhood or that being a mother is a woman's highest calling. Given the amount of attention the topic has generated over the years, you would expect there to be a score of Scriptures supporting the oft-taught conclusions that a woman's ultimate purpose is to be a helpmeet to her husband and bear children. The lack of Scriptures that speak to women's roles, let alone parenting, is truly astounding.

What I further realized is that, if I was going to be wise and responsible in discerning the meaning of different passages of Scripture, I needed to consider the few that speak to women's roles within the larger context of the patriarchal times in which they were written. Over the years various Bible theologians have studied these passages without agreeing on their meaning, but context gave me clues that my original understanding of biblical womanhood was far too limited. One much-touted example is the Proverbs 31 woman (also known as the "virtuous woman" or the "wife of noble character"), who has been propped up as the ultimate biblical role model for Christian women because of her domesticity and her devotion to her husband and children.

But what we can too easily miss is how extraordinary this woman is *beyond* marriage and motherhood. When was the last time you heard someone highlight the fact that she runs a business selling linen garments (verse 24) and ensures her trading is profitable (verse 18)? Or that she dabbles in real estate and uses the earnings to plant a vineyard (verse 16)? Or that she prioritizes caring for those in need in addition to caring for her family (verse 20)? Or that she has servant girls to help her on the home front (verse 15)? And never mind that she isn't even an actual woman who existed but rather a list of idealized attributes in the form of an acrostic poem thought to be recited by pious Jews of the day!

My point is that many of the positions we've been taught related to the roles of women often rely on isolated Bible verses taken out of the context of the whole of Scripture or the time they were written (and the cultural norms of the day). When this happens, we create burdens for ourselves and others that God never intended for us to carry.

One of my greatest joys in life has been being a mother. While I consider it an important calling, it is not my highest calling. Nor is it yours. And that should come as a great relief.

RETHINKING THE FAIRY TALE

Many of us would admit to, at some level, dreaming about the fairy tale—the prince, the castle, and eventually, the laughter of little royal offspring echoing through the corridors. We can blame it on chick flicks, romance novels, or our mothers (who, by simply being mothers, get blamed for almost everything). Oh, sure, we are products of our environment, but I also believe we enter the world hardwired to want what every fairy tale offers: a life of *happily ever after*. Disney movies and sappy song lyrics play on that desire, exploiting our vulnerable yearning to be *complete.*

In my treasure trove of keepsakes, I have a checklist my daughter handed me when she was just seven years old:

> Someday I will marry a man who is . ♡
>
> 1. is a cristen
> 2. has blue eyes
> 3. is a Longhorn

Despite coming from a long line of University of Texas Longhorns and college-football brainwashing from birth, my daughter ended up going to Auburn University, where she did, in fact, meet her future husband (who, for the record, has green eyes). But if my son-in-law was going to match only one-third of my daughter's fairy-tale wish list, at least he got the most important one right. (And thanks to a quality education, I'm happy to report that my daughter can now spell *Christian*.)

My daughter's fairy-tale pursuit was off to a good start. Within a year of getting married, she and her husband bought their first "castle" and decided to officially start trying to build their family.

For as long as I can remember, my daughter has wanted to be a mother. She tended to her dolls as a young mother-in-training. She staged mock weddings with neighbor boys and played pretend house for hours at a time. She talked about how many children she was going to have one day and what their names would be. And throughout her childhood, I reinforced the teaching that marriage and motherhood were key factors in the happily-ever-after formula of biblical womanhood.

I could not have imagined at the time that her future fairy tale would not play out as scripted. After a year of trying to get pregnant, my daughter was diagnosed with unexplained infertility. Another two years went by, years of back-to-back appointments and procedures with a fertility specialist. Watching my daughter and son-in-law suffer one heartbreak after another was unbearable. At one point, while my daughter and her husband were living with us for a short time before moving into a new home, my oldest son and his wife discovered they were expecting their second child. Knowing how difficult it would be for my daughter to hear the news, they asked me to tell her.

I will never forget the scene. As I entered my daughter's room and saw her sitting on her childhood bed, I had a flashback to her as a small child, tucking in her dolls and stuffed animals for the night. When I told her the news, the dam broke, and she collapsed in my arms. I sobbed along with her. As I attempted to comfort my daughter in her grief, I fumbled with the right words to say. I tried to reassure her that she had value and worth apart from motherhood and that her happiness did not depend on her ability to bear children. But as I spoke these words, I struggled to believe them. Could *I* have been happy had I not married or had children?

In my years of ministry, I had taught that Jesus alone satisfies our souls and had warned others against finding their worth and value in anything other than Christ. Yet as I comforted my daughter, I was forced to confront the reality that I wasn't sure I really believed, deep down, that Jesus alone was *enough*.

Seeing my daughter's pain as she attempted to reconcile whether her life could have purpose without children shook me to the core. That night I confessed to her my own wrestlings over what I'd been taught regarding a woman's ultimate purpose. I apologized for imparting the false teaching that a woman's happiness is tethered to marriage and motherhood. Somewhere along the way, I had believed a lie, and sadly, I had taught her to believe it too.

There is nothing wrong with dreaming about marriage and motherhood. There is nothing wrong with finding joy and meaning in those things. I love being a mother. Raising my children has been one of the greatest joys of my life. But we must quit declaring motherhood to be a woman's highest calling and conflating it with a woman's ultimate purpose. You are more than a wife. You are more than a mom. You are first and foremost a child of God. Nowhere in the Bible does it say your worth is directly linked to a life role you may or may not play.

When we list marriage and motherhood as key components of biblical womanhood, we suggest that women who do not marry or have children are somehow unbiblical. Even worse, connecting these roles to womanhood in general suggests that women who don't marry or have children are lacking the defining characteristics of being a woman. Likewise, if motherhood is a woman's highest calling, does that mean that women who aren't mothers are, by default, relegated to some lesser calling in life? Do they have less value in the eyes of God?

Of course not! Our identity is rooted in who we are in Christ, not in what we do or a role we have.

Sadly, a recent study found that 35 percent of mothers described being a parent as the single most important aspect of their personhood.[2] This is not surprising, given the emphasis in our culture on making our children the center of our lives. Being a mother may be an aspect of who we are as women, but it is not our primary identity.

When motherhood becomes our primary identity, we have made it into an idol. In his book *Counterfeit Gods*, the late Timothy Keller writes, "An idol is whatever you look at and say, in your heart of hearts, 'If I have that, then I'll feel my life has meaning, then I'll know I have value, then I'll feel significant and secure.'"[3] The sobering truth about idols is that they always disappoint. If we rely on motherhood to give our lives meaning, make us feel valued, and help us feel significant and secure, we're going to quickly find ourselves scrambling to do everything right to avoid any feelings of failure. When we mess up, we're more likely to try to explain it away or to hide in shame. When our kids make painful choices, we're more likely to experience a deep personal shame that we project outward to our kids or become so obsessed with fixing the problems that we introduce unhealthy codependency into the mix. Motherhood, like anything else we make into an idol, will not deliver the true satisfaction our hearts seek—satisfaction found only in Christ.

MISTAKEN IDENTITY

If I asked you the question *Who are you?* and gave you thirty seconds to answer, what would you say? Would you talk about a role you play? A job title you have? Qualities you possess? Accolades you have earned? How likely would it be for the word *mother* to be in your answer?

Of course, motherhood can be a huge part of who we are, but it does not define our true identity. At our very core, we are beloved children of God. Why, then, do so many Christian women mistakenly link their identity to their status as a mother?

Even despite outside societal pressures and spiritual expectations within the church at-large, most of us as Christians know the biblical answer to the question of our true identity—but we usually struggle to practice it. How do I know this? Because I've been this woman. (Knowing the right answer doesn't automatically mean we live from the truth.)

Almost every book and Bible study I've written to women and girls over the years contains a specific passage of Scripture that has been revolutionary in reminding me where my identity lies and, most importantly, where I can find the only source of *enough*. When I find myself retreating to the same dysfunctional patterns, looking for worth and value in all the wrong places, I preach this passage from Ephesians 3 back to myself over and over. I'll ask you to read through it slowly and soak it in:

> I pray that from his glorious, unlimited resources
> he will empower you with inner strength through
> his Spirit. Then Christ will make his home in your

hearts as you trust in him. Your roots will grow down into God's love and keep you strong. And may you have the power to understand, as all God's people should, how wide, how long, how high, and how deep his love is. May you experience the love of Christ, though it is too great to understand fully. Then you will be made complete with all the fullness of life and power that comes from God.
EPHESIANS 3:16-19, NLT

In this beautiful prayer, as the apostle Paul prays for Jewish and Gentile believers, he acknowledges that the source of inner strength is from the Holy Spirit, who dwells in the hearts of God's people. When we're in the habit of relying on the Holy Spirit for inner strength, Paul tells us, we see ourselves and the world through a different lens. That's because Christ is at home in our hearts, deeply rooted in our lives.[4]

But it's difficult to base our identity and worth on the status of *being* a child of God when we live in a world that links identity and worth to doing and performing. The truth is that many of us moms are accustomed to relying on our own strength to solve our problems. That's one of the dangers in centering our identity on motherhood: We become so focused on doing everything perfectly that we forget we're not the ones in charge of the outcome.

Paul acknowledges in this passage that the love of Christ is too great to understand fully, which is why following him is an act of growing deep roots and actively dwelling in his love. The problem is, most of us fail to dwell in Christ's love and instead jump right back into our performance-based rituals to satisfy the ache in our souls.

Christ is not content to be on the fringes of our lives, an afterthought in times of need. He wants to be at the absolute center of our lives. As we become more rooted and established in his immense love for us, we will finally experience what our hearts truly long for—to "be made complete with all the fullness of life and power that comes from God" (Ephesians 3:19, NLT). This is our identity. This is what moves us from striving to be *enough* to living confidently in being *already good enough*.

The Greek word translated "made complete" in this verse is *plēróō*, and it means "to fill (a container)," or we might say "level up (a hollow thing)."[5] Our deepest desire is to level up the hollow places in our hearts. As fulfilling as motherhood can be, it is not enough to satisfy or complete us. Our hearts were wired for God.

He is the only one who can level up the hollow thing and satisfy our souls. Nothing else will do.

Let's lay aside the false belief that everything depends on us getting motherhood right. Let's remember our identity as God's children, deeply and unconditionally loved. Only then will we be able to rely on Christ to get us through each day, one challenge at a time. Only when we know who we are will we know whose we are.*

---

* Entire books have been written on our identity in Christ, but I have included several verses in the appendix that directly speak to who we are in Christ. I encourage you to meditate on them and even commit them to memory if you struggle with mistaken identity.

LIVING LIFE ON PURPOSE

How does our identity in Christ reshape our understanding of ourselves and our purpose in life? How does that change our approach to motherhood? Once we understand the foundation of our identity, we are better equipped to walk in our ultimate purpose.

Do you believe you have a purpose in this world? Sadly, one research survey found that "less than one in five moms (19%) [say] they regularly feel they are 'able to contribute meaningfully to the world.'"[6] I suspect one reason for this heartbreaking statistic is that mothers are told they should accomplish far more than Christ commanded when it comes to their life purpose. It's no wonder so many of us feel we are always coming up short.

The purpose we are invited into is no different from that of any human being, regardless of role, gender, age, ethnicity, or status—and to learn about it, there is no better source to go to than Jesus himself. When asked by a Pharisee, "Teacher, which is the greatest commandment in the Law?" Jesus does not break his answer down into gender-assigned duties and distinct roles for men and women. Rather, he replies,

> "'Love the Lord your God with all your heart and with all your soul and with all your mind.' This is the first and greatest commandment. And the second is like it: 'Love your neighbor as yourself.' All the Law and the Prophets hang on these two commandments."
>
> MATTHEW 22:36-40

As part of our purpose, we are called to love God with all our hearts, souls, and minds. Loving God was never meant to be a duty or a chore but rather a natural by-product of having first been loved by God.

All too often, loving God has been reduced to a chore or spiritual discipline. When I was a young mother, I was also a fairly new believer. I benefited greatly from a small group that was led by an older, godly Christian woman who drilled home the importance of a daily quiet time—basically, spending time in God's Word and prayer. When we would meet as a group, she would ask at the beginning how we were doing with our daily quiet times. While I understand the sentiment of encouraging this discipline, I began to equate loving God to time spent reading the Bible and praying. In other words, completing a checklist of tasks was tangible evidence that I loved God. When I missed a day or more, I felt like a failure as a Christian and imagined God shaking his head with a low-level sense of displeasure and disappointment. Ironically, the more I saw God through that lens, the less I wanted to spend time with him!

Life with God was never meant to be this complicated. He is not logging quiet-time attendance on a chart or weighing your love for him on a scale.

> This is love: not that we loved God, but that he loved us and sent his Son as an atoning sacrifice for our sins.
> 1 JOHN 4:10

> We love because he first loved us.
> 1 JOHN 4:19

We can't help but love God when we dwell first on the love he has for us.

The love that defines us and motivates us, that keeps us connected to God and shapes how we relate to everyone around us, spills over into every part of our lives. And motherhood is one of those places.

Let me say that again: We don't start with *How can I be the best mother?* Motherhood and parenting aren't the first priorities. Our identity, based on being rooted and established in the love of Christ, is the first priority; motherhood is one of the ways we live out this primary identity. In fact, we see this exact thing when Jesus is informing the Pharisee of the greatest commandment. Jesus is giving a nod to the Shema in Deuteronomy 6, a declaration and prayer that ancient Israelites recited daily and many practicing Jews still recite today:

> Hear, O Israel: The LORD our God, the LORD is one. Love the LORD your God with all your heart and with all your soul and with all your strength. These commandments that I give you today are to be on your hearts. Impress them on your children. Talk about them when you sit at home and when you walk along the road, when you lie down and when you get up.
> **DEUTERONOMY 6:4-7**

This Deuteronomy 6 passage is one of few in the Bible that address parenting directly. But look at the order of this passage: As important as it is to impress God's commandments on our children's hearts, the Shema begins with who God is and with our primary identity as people who dwell in God's love. As we grow in our love for God (with heart, soul, mind, and strength), the logical by-product will be a desire to share his love with others. Our universal purpose as believers is to spread the Good News of his gospel (Matthew 28:19-20; Mark 16:15-16; Luke 14:23; Acts 1:7-8). We should live out our callings in such a way that we are seeking to know God and make him known in every realm of our lives.

Once again, you cannot make known what you do not personally know. This is why establishing our identity in Christ is essential. As we dwell in his love, it is impossible not to want to share that love with others. When Jesus gave his final earthly charge—best known as the great commission—to his eleven disciples, he didn't say, "Therefore go and tell the people to get married and make babies," as if populating the earth were our greatest responsibility. Nor did he designate gender-specific callings. His charge to his remaining disciples is his universal charge to all his followers: "Go and make disciples" (Matthew 28:19).

In 2 Corinthians, Paul lays out our calling in greater detail:

> All this is from God, who reconciled us to himself through Christ and gave us the ministry of reconciliation: that God was reconciling the world to himself in Christ, not counting people's sins against them. And he has committed to us the message of reconciliation. We are therefore Christ's ambassadors, as though God were making his appeal

through us. We implore you on Christ's behalf: Be reconciled to God.

2 CORINTHIANS 5:18-20

Did you catch that? We have been given a ministry! Thus, we are ministers who have been given the awesome privilege of partnering with God to share the Good News that God is no longer counting people's sins against them. Paul then gives us a title: "Christ's ambassadors." The Greek word translated "ambassador" in this passage is *presbeuō*, which generally refers to a respected (often elderly) representative.[7] We are called to be Christ's representatives to any and all within our spheres of influence. Again, had it been important to designate gender-related roles, Paul could have given this ministry call exclusively to the men and added a footnote to indicate "unless you are a woman, and then your ministry is only to your husband and children."

The truth is that we've made this far too complicated. We're defining our value, purpose, and worth through the wrong lens. I'm not talking about adding more to our plates but rather readjusting our definition of value and purpose as it relates to God's calling on our lives: discovering our identity as *ministers* rather than as *mothers*.

Let me ask you this: Do you think of yourself as first and foremost a *minister* or a *mother*? You are assigned your life purpose when you become a believer, not when you become a mother. Our role as mothers is encompassed within our calling as ministers. Your children are part of the ministry assignment you are called to, and while being a mother is an important role, it is not your only role.

Most Christian mothers are doing an amazing job fulfilling their roles as ministers to their children. They make countless holy deposits in the lives of their children on a daily basis, whether it's guiding them in bedtime prayers, leading family devotions, taking them to church, teaching them about God and his love, training them to make wise and biblical choices, raising them to love others and treat one another as fellow image bearers of God, modeling love for the Bible and its commandments, or pointing to nature and the beauty that surrounds us as evidence of God.

But our calling expands far beyond the walls of our homes. What an honor it is that Christ invites us to play any part in his Kingdom purposes! Whether you are married, single, a mom, a grandmother, an aunt, a coworker, a friend, a student, or quite simply a follower of Christ, you are meant to fulfill your calling in your church, neighborhood, workplace, school, ballpark, extracurricular activities, and community as you go, in every chapter of your life.

Yes, in the busy years of raising children, it can feel overwhelming to expand our ministry beyond the demands on the home front. We often conflate ministry with preaching, teaching, and serving, but it is so much more. On some days, your ministry may be a simple prayer for a friend who is in need. It can be an offer to watch the child of an overwhelmed mother and receiving the same help yourself when needed. It can be a text to someone God places on your heart to let them know you are thinking about them. It can be the confident encouragement to those in your sphere that Christ is worthy of our trust and desires relationships with us.

As you live out the beauty of the gospel in your own life and become entrenched in God's immense love, your life will become your ministry. The fruit of the Spirit—love, joy, peace, patience, kindness, goodness, faithfulness, gentleness, and self-control (Galatians 5:22-23)—will be evident and offer hope to others who desire to know the source. When you mess up, your humility, vulnerability, and ultimate security that you are unconditionally loved by God will be contagious to others who long for that kind of love and acceptance. Ministry is not always *sharing* the power of the gospel but also *showing* the power of the gospel.

AN EMPTY-NEST PERSPECTIVE

While scrolling my social-media feed one day, a reel popped up of a popular parenting influencer who treated their followers to a spontaneous video tour of their messy home. I suppose the goal was to help normalize the reality of raising children. As the parent walked through the living room, they navigated an obstacle course of toys strewn across the floor. Then they made their way to the kitchen, offering a glimpse of dirty dishes piled up in the kitchen sink. Finally, the camera turned to the washroom and its pile of dirty laundry the size of Mount Everest on the floor. The simple caption read,

> Let this reel remind you to live in the moment, with the mess and chaos and dirty laundry. It won't always be like that . . . and that should break your heart.[8]

Hmm, I thought, glancing around at my post-empty-nest living room, clear of toys and clutter, as I sat on my well-earned cream-colored sofa free from toddler fingerprints, smudges, and stains. While I understood the sentiment of the post and would endorse the advice to "live in the moment, with the mess and chaos and dirty laundry," I didn't feel heartbroken over the absence of it all. I may miss certain moments of raising my children, but I'm also celebrating the stage I'm in. I earned my stripes. The empty-nest chapter isn't a heartbreaking and dreaded reality of life after children—it's a reward.

Curious, I scrolled down to the comments to see whether anyone shared my perspective. One mother of young children had the courage to weigh in and admit that while she loves her children very much and sees it as "an honor to be their mother," she is also looking forward to the years when she can have more time to herself. She explained that her philosophy is to find happiness in each chapter of her life and not look to her children to provide that happiness. "Instead of being nostalgic over the absence of my children," she wrote, "I plan to enjoy my life in the future (without the messy toys and chaos)."

Sounded like a reasonable and emotionally healthy response to me! But it didn't go over well with some of the commenters. One simply replied, "I feel sorry for you." Another one chimed in, "Feeling so sad for your kids right now." And another: "Sorry but I think you have a problem." And another: "Go to therapy." And possibly the worst: "I pity your children that they have a mother such as yourself."

You would have thought by reading their comments that this mother had advocated for sending her children to a wilderness boot camp until they turned eighteen. Apparently you can't express a desire to have a life beyond your children on social media without an angry-mom mob coming for you. I shook my head in disbelief and felt sadness for the mother who was the target of their bullying. But I also felt a tremendous sadness for the mothers whose entire lives are defined by their status and role. The empty-nest years are going to be a rude awakening as they struggle to figure out who they are in the aftermath of their children leaving home.

I have witnessed this reality firsthand among many women my age. In that very social-media post, a few older empty-nest moms had commented an amen to the original sentiment, some saying they would give anything to go back to the days of raising their children, messes and all. I wasn't really surprised. My generation embraced a child-centric brand of parenting, and many mothers tethered their identity and purpose to motherhood. Once the children were gone—and along with them, the never-ending list of responsibilities and activities revolving around their children's lives and schedules—these women felt completely lost.

Some reacted to the shock by inserting themselves into their adult children's lives—attempting to manage their college schedules, trying to oversee their activities from afar, and having unrealistic expectations about involvement in their lives even after marriage. Others sunk into a deep depression, numb and unsure how to navigate the future. Sadly, yet others separated from or divorced their husbands due to a lack of common interests, oftentimes because they had long prioritized their children over their marriage.

I want to camp out on this point for a minute. We've already discussed the issues with tying our identity to motherhood rather than living out of our identity in Christ. But another danger with making motherhood our identity is that it disrupts the way God created marriage to work. "Leave and cleave" isn't just about preparing our kids for marriage; if we are married, it should remain the first reality in our marriages as well.

In his book *The Meaning of Marriage,* Timothy Keller writes that God "didn't put a parent and a child in the Garden" but "a husband and a wife. When you marry your spouse, that must supersede all other relationships, even the parental relationship. Your spouse and your marriage must be the number one priority in your life."[9]

Sadly, many Christian families have bought into the lie that the needs, wants, and desires of the children should come before the needs, wants, and desires of the parents. Kid-centric homes have become the norm in our culture. Several years ago, a Christian woman told me she and her husband hadn't been on a single date since marrying; instead, they do "family nights." Of course, there is nothing wrong with having family nights. But family nights do not prioritize the marriage—they prioritize the children. And if you only prioritize your children, you will find yourself, after your last child flies the nest, waking up to a virtual stranger every morning. It's not a coincidence that the divorce rate for couples over fifty has quadrupled over the last thirty years.[10]

I'm not saying this to shame anyone. I know how loud the never-ending needs of kids can be and how easy it is to push the relatively quieter needs of a marriage to the back burner. Shortly after my husband and I married, we found out we were (unexpectedly!) expecting our first child. Our one-year anniversary was spent at a Lamaze childbirth class. Exactly thirteen months after our wedding day, our son was born, and instantaneously our identities shifted to *Mom* and *Dad*. Two more children followed, and sleepless nights and colicky infants replaced date nights and adult conversations. In those early, comatose years, we told ourselves that someday, when the children weren't so dependent on us, we'd have time to focus on being a couple again. But *someday* never seemed to arrive.

By our six-year anniversary, we had a five-year-old, a three-year-old, and a newborn. Even amid the noise and chaos of three young children, we both felt desperately alone. By the eight-year mark, my husband and I landed in a counselor's office with our marriage on life support.

By far, one of the best takeaways we learned during our counseling sessions was the importance of scheduling regular, consistent date nights. Date nights had been one of the first things to go when we'd become new parents. Aside from the fact that it was costly to get a babysitter and go out to dinner, it was impossible to get out the door without the kids melting down in the background. Year after year, we made excuses. Without a designated date night that focused on our marriage, the kids became our common bond. They were the topic of 99 percent of our conversations. Our counselor encouraged us to start dating again (and suggested not talking about our children on our dates!) to rebuild our friendship. Without a friendship as the foundation, true intimacy—the kind God intends for marriage—would not be possible.

Our weekly dates helped us realize how much we had missed each other. We started laughing again and having fun. We began acting like a married couple rather than two people who happened to live in the same house and parent the same children. And in the process, we became better parents and modeled what a healthy marriage looks like to our children.

My husband and I are a couple of years shy of our fortieth wedding anniversary, and he is truly my best friend. We love doing life together. I can't imagine where we'd be if we hadn't taken the time to rebuild our marriage and, more importantly, our friendship. Now, with our children grown and gone, we see the value of the investment we made to nurture our marriage in the earlier years.

There's a lot of negative press about the empty-nest years, especially among Christian mothers. It saddens me to hear young mothers speak of it with dread. And it certainly doesn't help to hear older women my age echo, "Enjoy it while you can—you will miss this stage when they're gone" or "These are the best years of your life—it's never quite the same once the children leave." But an empty-nest perspective equips us to make decisions today for a healthy, life-giving future—for us, for our husbands, and for our children.

With an empty-nest perspective, you remember that your children are not yours to keep. You invest in your friendship with your husband, the person who will live with you far longer than your children do. You cultivate a perspective, identity, and rhythm of life that equips you to know who you are and find purpose and delight in the post-child years.

If you have embraced the truth that you are more than a mom, you will learn how to live at peace with the lopsided love of the parent-child relationship. Children will never love their parents in the same way their parents love them. We pour into them, nurture them, love them, train them, guide them, and then release them to go and do likewise if they marry and have children. If this makes you sad or anxious or upset, please know that I am not telling you this to stir up your emotions. I am encouraging you to discover who you are apart from being a mother, because a day will come when your job will be complete. This is God's plan, and it is healthy to keep that in the forefront of our minds.

As someone who found great joy in mothering my children, I can speak firsthand to the benefit of having an empty-nest perspective along the way. Letting go of something you love is never easy. New normals always come with learning curves. Knowing who you are in Christ, walking in your God-given purpose, and remembering that you are more than a mom will make the transition much easier.

REFLECTION QUESTIONS

1. In what ways did you buy into the fairy tale that marriage and motherhood are key components to a life lived "happily ever after"? What role did marriage and motherhood play in your understanding of biblical womanhood?

2. When it comes to your identity, how much does motherhood play into your primary identity? How would you answer the question *Who are you?* How does the biblical truth of who you are in Christ show up in your everyday life?

3. When it comes to your ultimate purpose, do you see yourself as more of a *minister* or a *mother*? How might you walk more intentionally in your calling as a minister first? How does that calling encompass your role as a mother?

4. How might having an empty-nest perspective help you redefine your God-given identity and purpose?

TWO

CANCEL THE GUILT TRIP

The Grace of Being Imperfect

> There is therefore now no condemnation to them which are in Christ Jesus.
> **ROMANS 8:1, KJV**

It was the last week of my senior year of high school, and I was sitting on the gym bleachers among my peers. We were gathered for Senior Awards Day, where those who had excelled in academics, sports, and school-sponsored clubs would be recognized and applauded. I was a good student and involved in many activities, but I doubted I'd be up for any awards (unless there was one for talking too much in class). I had already been accepted to the college of my choice, so I didn't think much about it at the time. As the ceremony progressed, I marveled at the students whose names were called over and over. I didn't recognize many of them, even though we'd spent four years together in the same school. I don't recall seeing them at Friday-night games, school dances, parties, or other social hangouts. While I was busy having fun and hanging out with friends, they were focused on the future and making sacrifices along the way.

Truthfully, *good enough* was just fine with me. It was enough to get me through college, find a job, and meet the man of my dreams. Why make all the sacrifices to obtain top-tier excellence if at the end of the day most of us land in the same place? *Good enough* seemed to be more my style and my pace, or so I reasoned at the time.

That is, until I became a mother.

From the moment I saw the positive pink line on the pregnancy test, I knew *good enough* would not do. While the philosophy had served me well, my children deserved better. It was no longer about *my* personal well-being or *my* future—now I was on the hook for theirs as well. Top quarter was not good enough. Top ten was not good enough. If there was a valedictorian of motherhood, that was the aim. My children deserved nothing short of perfect. It wasn't about a prize, a pat on the back, or accolades for me. The ultimate prize at the end of this pursuit was to raise happy, healthy, well-adjusted children who loved and followed Jesus Christ. That one pink line awakened me to the overwhelming responsibility of nurturing and caring for someone other than myself. I was going to rise to the occasion, even if it meant sacrificing my own well-being in the process. Society expected it of me. The church expected it of me. And most of all, I expected it of myself.

It's been nearly four decades since I glanced at that first pregnancy test and decided that *good enough* wouldn't cut it as a mother. And still I never felt like I was doing an exceptional job. Motherhood proved far more difficult than I'd imagined. What worked for one child didn't necessarily work for my other children. The rules were always changing, and the expectations along with them. There was no foolproof formula when it came to raising children; there were no guarantees.

Truth be told, on most days I felt like a failure. I felt like I was barely scraping by, my greatest achievement being that I'd kept the kids alive another day. Rather than aiming for the pinnacle of exceptional, I felt like reality was a downgraded, internalized standard of pass-fail. I felt my report card was stamped with "needs improvement" in just about every category of motherhood. Somehow, despite my inadequacies and shortcomings, I managed to raise three happy, healthy, well-adjusted children who grew up to love and follow Jesus Christ. (But let me also say that a child's faith or lack thereof is not a marker of a parent's success or failure. I know plenty of Christian parents who have done a phenomenal job of passing their faith on to their children only to have their children reject that faith. In the end, it is up to our children to decide whether to follow Christ.)

Motherhood, evolving and highly unpredictable as it is, is not for the faint of heart. Try as you may, you will not be able to control unknown variables. There will be sick children, canceled vacations, unforeseen expenses, sibling rivalry, incessant whining, plenty of boo-boos, shrill screams that make your ears ring, crying at the drop of a pin, broken hearts, back talk, teenage rebellion, missed curfews, stained carpet and upholstery, mental-health challenges, food battles, shouting matches over screen time, and plenty of marital arguments when you and your husband don't align on the issues at hand. You will lose your cool, say things you regret, and at times want to hand in your notice. Never mind that often times you will be juggling any number of parenting challenges while also facing personal challenges.

This is the reality of parenthood. All the above is perfectly normal. What is not normal is to wake up and expect each day to go smoothly, without any hitches or glitches. In fact, the smooth days will be the exception. The proverbial supermom who does it all and does it well is an illusion. If you are to find relief from the overexpectations of twenty-first-century motherhood, you must let go of the idea that perfection is possible. It doesn't matter how many parenting books or articles you read, how many courses you take, or how many mom influencers you follow for advice—motherhood will be hard. Often extremely hard. The sooner you accept this truth, the sooner you will regain your sanity. Because when "I can't get anything wrong" is what drives you, the inevitable guilt that follows will crush you when you get something wrong. And it's only a matter of time until that happens.

THE ENEMY OF GOOD

> I am shattered. After weeks of trying everything possible to get my baby to properly latch and nurse, I finally had to give it up. On top of that, the baby had lost weight, and when I took him in for his checkup, the pediatrician made me feel even more guilty than I already felt (as if that's even possible) because I'd

waited so long to switch to formula. I have cried so many tears over this. I feel like I have already failed my child, and he's not even a month old!¹

When I read these words from a young mom on social media, my heart ached for her—not so much because her breastfeeding attempts had failed but because of the burden of guilt she carried for a situation outside her control. She explained elsewhere in the post that she had met with numerous lactation specialists, tried every tip and trick imaginable, and suffered through a case of mastitis in her attempts to get her child to nurse. The fact that she felt a need to defend her decision to formula-feed spoke volumes about the pressure of motherhood expectations. I wanted to wrap her in my arms and tell her, "It is okay. You are a fabulous mother, and you have not failed your son. One day you will look back and this will all be a blur. Your only regret will be that you didn't extend more grace and compassion to yourself in that moment." Sadly, I knew it wouldn't be her last guilt trip. Guilt trips are guaranteed when we make our motherhood gold standard *I can't get anything wrong.*

I could fill a book with stories of the guilt trips I've taken over the years. I felt so much guilt when I began dropping my firstborn off to a twice-a-week preschool program shortly after his sister was born. I peeled him off my leg at the doorway of his class and heard him shriek "Mommmmmmy!" as I exited the building—then collapsed in my car and sobbed the whole way home. At times I gave in and loaded him back in the car. The guilt was just too heavy.

Or there was the time my youngest son was doing forward rolls on the sofa and fell off and hurt his wrist. He was a toddler and seemed to shake it off at the time, but when he was still avoiding using that hand two days later, I took him to the doctor. An X-ray showed a hairline fracture, and I felt like the worst mother on the planet.

Or I think about the time my daughter tried out for cheerleader at the end of her freshman year and I was out of town that day for a speaking engagement. She called me in tears after tryouts that morning to say she had messed up on one of the cheers and was certain she wouldn't make the team. She wanted me to come get her from school. I beat myself up all day for being out of town. Then, when she made the squad, I felt guilty I wasn't there to celebrate with her after she found out!

Guilt is "a feeling of responsibility or remorse for some offense, crime, wrong, etc., whether real or imagined."[2] When guilt is healthy (or "true"), it's accurately pointing us to a wrongdoing in our conscience, prompting us toward sorrow, repentance, and a change in behavior. But the actions or inactions that lead to feelings of guilt can be subjective. Not every pang of guilt signals a wrongdoing.

When guilt is unhealthy (or "false"), it is not pointing us to a wrongdoing but rather the inability to meet an unreasonable standard due to circumstances beyond our control. This standard can be self-imposed or an outside expectation. Even though we haven't done anything wrong, we feel responsible for the result. The problem is that many mothers, just because they want to be the best mothers possible to their children, internalize *false guilt* as *true guilt*.

False guilt is impossible to resolve. You can't confess something you didn't intend to do. You can't repent of something that is not wrong. You can't fix something outside your control. You can't predict the future, control unforeseen circumstances, be present (literally or figuratively) in all situations, or know all there is to know about any given situation or event that occurs or may occur. False guilt always points a finger of blame—you should have known, should have been there, should have responded differently, and should always be able to fix the problem. It is based on a distorted perspective that assumes a divine, godlike perfection.

Fortunately, God doesn't expect us to be God. That job is already taken. We are mere humans, and we come with limitations.

LIES AND TRUTH

Each of us is vulnerable to the pressures of unrealistic motherhood expectations—and the guilt that invariably follows. Some mothers may have felt neglected or invisible in their own childhoods and as a result seek to offer their children the childhoods they longed for. Others are perfectionists by nature and strive for excellence in everything they pursue. They've been aiming for A+ their entire lives, so *average* is not in their vocabularies. Yet others saw a wonderful example of parents who modeled a healthy home-life balance—and think replicating that perfectly is the only way to parent well.

Regardless of the backstory, most mothers simply want to offer their children the very best. They don't want to let them down. As a result, they develop their own mental list of "good mother" expectations:

- *Good mothers sign their children up for _____.*
- *Good mothers live in their cars, shuttling their children to various activities that promise to enrich their lives.*
- *Good mothers are always mindful of nutrition and make as much as possible from scratch.*
- *Good mothers raise well-mannered, obedient children.*
- *Good mothers live in clutter-free homes.*
- *Good mothers expose their children to as many experiences as possible to help them identify their gifts and talents.*
- *Good mothers spend hours each day playing with or teaching their children to help them get ahead in life.*
- *Good mothers work long hours to afford private school and summer camps.*
- *Good mothers never miss a game or school event.*
- *Good mothers never complain, regardless of how exhausted they are.*
- *Good mothers _____.*

It's not just that we don't want to let our children down—we don't want to let ourselves down. In a way, we seek to fulfill as many "good mother" expectations as we can to guard against future regret. After all, if we get everything right now, we won't feel like a failure later, right?

But is it possible that in our attempt to guard against the future regret of not *doing enough* and *being enough* we will instead be left with regret that we tried to do *too much*? How much of the anxiety in parents and children can be traced to a deep sense that, try as we may, we will never measure up to the expectations around us?

Let me be honest. When the pursuit to achieve this "good mother" status requires us to meet endless metrics that extend beyond any reasonable human capacity—we need to start asking ourselves what is true and what are lies. Because a lot of the guilt we carry comes from the lies we are told, and more importantly, the lies we come to believe.

Imagine if you kept a motherhood guilt journal over the course of a one-week period. In fact, I encourage you to try it—log every time you feel a pang of motherhood guilt as a way to gauge how often motherhood guilt affects you on a daily basis. As you do, you'll probably begin to see some patterns—and chances are good that many of the guilt traps you experience can be traced back to a lie you have come to believe is true.

Here are some of the common lies that often lead mothers into debilitating guilt traps—and the corresponding truths that can help us break free:

- **Lie:** *There is one perfect way to parent.*
- **Truth:** At face value, this seems like an obvious lie. But while we know deep down that there is no one way to parent, we often live very differently. We crave security, consistency, and certainty—but parenting thrusts us into a realm of chronic insecurity, inconsistency, and

uncertainty. Often we try to create security and regain control by adopting black-and-white positions. All the while, we find ourselves constantly bombarded with strong opinions from other moms and online experts who provide little nuance about parenting decisions. Bedtime at 7:00 p.m. until age ten, no exceptions. No smartphone until age sixteen, no exceptions. No dinner until chores are done, no exceptions. No sibling fights, no exceptions. If only it were so simple (especially the sibling fights!). Guilt ensues when our black-and-white approach fails and we begin to question whether we are parenting the "right" way or the "wrong" way. The truth is that we learn what works best for each child in each season as we go. Parenting is a journey, and what works for one family, one context, or one child may not work for another.

- **Lie:** *You owe it to your child to give them the best of everything.*
- **Truth:** It's perfectly natural to want to give your children the very best. But fulfilling their every desire can produce spoiled, entitled children who become spoiled, entitled adults. Likewise, fulfilling their every want and need will produce children who expect others in their lives to do the same. Sadly, the greatest dose of guilt stemming from this lie can often come from our children as they compare their lives with the lives of their peers. Of course they want the latest smartphone or

tablet, the name-brand clothes and pricey tennis shoes, the spring-break beach vacations and summer camps, a car when they turn sixteen—and the list goes on. If we're honest, many of us can admit to having the same struggle: comparing our lives to others' and wanting what we don't have. They can be valuable teaching moments when we are open and honest with our children about the struggle with comparison as well as the need to be grateful for what we have.

- **Lie:** *You should never be tired, have an off day, or feel like giving up.*
- **Truth:** Motherhood can be extremely exhausting, both mentally and physically. Not every aspect of motherhood is joyful. There will be many days you feel like quitting. It is perfectly normal to feel this way. Just as you might discuss "highs and lows" with your children, you need to extend the same grace to yourself. It's healthy for your children to see that their mother also has "highs and lows" and sometimes needs a break—even if that break is from them!

- **Lie:** *You should always know if your child is struggling developmentally, emotionally, physically, academically, or spiritually.*
- **Truth:** A mom friend of mine recently shared that she was struggling with guilt because her daughter, who is in high school, had recently been diagnosed with a

learning disability (dyslexia). She was beating herself up because her daughter is in a homeschool-hybrid program and she felt she should have recognized the warning signs earlier than she did since she is one of her daughter's teachers. Never mind that she also homeschools another child, volunteers many hours serving her church, and has no formal background in detecting learning disabilities. Even though we know our children better than most anyone else, we are not psychic. We can't possibly know everything there is to know about our children at any given moment in time. We can be diligently involved in our children's lives and encourage open communication and still miss that they may be struggling. We can't be responsible for what we don't know, aren't told, fail to see, or fail to understand.

- **Lie:** *A good mother does it all.*
- **Truth:** Every mom has strengths and weaknesses. No mother is good at everything (even if social media leads you to believe otherwise). Some mothers are creative and good at playing pretend or involving their children in art projects or outdoor play. Other mothers are gifted in scheduling and organization and offer structure to their children's lives. Yet others find joy in the kitchen and love to whip up home-cooked meals and snacks. Others are great at teaching their children and turning everyday activities into learning experiences. Others are good at creating special memories, whether it's with birthday traditions, Bible verses, notes on their children's bathroom

mirrors, or spontaneous skip days to go to the park. Some mothers can juggle many things at once, while others prefer to focus on one event at a time.

You set yourself up for a guilt trap when you assume you must be all things to your child. Just as some things come easier and more naturally to your child and you work to cultivate their gifts, you have a unique bent and personality. Cultivate your gifts and mom style and let yourself off the hook of being good at everything. If you're not naturally suited to be a homeroom mom, don't do it. If you're asked to bring a treat for your child's class party but you don't enjoy baking, pick it up at the store. And if you see a mom on social media post a picture of her child's first day of school with balloons, streamers, and a letter board marking the day and that's not your thing, shrug it off. Don't try to become someone you're not. You do you. God chose you to be your child's mother, which means your child needs you to bring your unique gifts and not try to be someone you're not. More importantly, you owe it to yourself to be yourself.

There is no perfect brand of motherhood. To embrace this false assumption is to set yourself up for failure every step of the way. All these lies fall under the bigger lie that as a mother you have to get it all right. There is no room for error. Too much is at stake. Your children are counting on you. But when this impossible standard is not met, the result will always be guilt.

I'm reminded of the guilt-laced words of one of my daughter's friends after she took her young son to a local coffee shop. He ate an unlabeled cake pop that appeared to be chocolate, but unfortunately, it contained peanut butter—and because he had a peanut allergy, he began to show signs of asphyxiation. The mother felt guilty that she hadn't asked questions in advance about the unlabeled cake pop or brought an EpiPen with her. "Two things I will never let happen again!" she said. Fortunately, someone in the store had an EpiPen; her son was transported to the hospital by ambulance as a precautionary measure and is perfectly fine.

As if her guilt over the event wasn't enough of a burden to carry, this mom got an extra heaping dose served up on a platter from the coffee-shop owner when she contacted him to encourage putting labels on items. Unfortunately, the owner immediately assumed a posture of callous defensiveness. When she asked him to put himself in her shoes as a parent, he replied, "You don't want to know what I would've done as a parent. I would've asked a million questions about the cake pop."

The assumption that mothers are supposed to get everything right all the time is so pervasive that we've come to expect it. And many of us expect it of ourselves. This lie is peddled by a variety of factors, including

- a culture that puts intense pressure on mothers to perform exceptionally in every facet of parenthood;
- advertising campaigns that are created to exploit a common fear in mothers that they'll let their kids down if

they don't do/buy such-and-such product or service to solve the problem;

- other mothers, family members, and friends who have their own dogmatic ideas of what motherhood should entail and which parenting philosophies are correct;

- churches and Christian communities who have placed unreasonable expectations on mothers to create homes that are peaceful and always tidy, to parent perfectly, to have well-behaved children, and to cultivate spiritual rhythms that ensure their children always make the right choices, just to name a few things;

- social-media parenting influencers who offer highlight reels of their lives, edited, filtered, and trimmed to perfection, oftentimes with an unseen staff helping peddle the illusion of seamless effortlessness; and

- coffee-shop owners who are all too eager to point out the ways we're falling short.

Motherhood is hard. You will make mistakes. You are not perfect. You are not psychic. You will have days when you want to give up. You are good at many things, but not everything. This is all perfectly normal. You are a wonderful mother just as you are and the exact mother God intended your children to have. Once you believe that, you will be able to guard against the expectations of those who tell you otherwise.

TRADING GUILT FOR GRACE

My youngest child was my largest baby, weighing in at slightly over nine pounds when he was born. But when he was a couple of weeks old, he suddenly began projectile vomiting and rapidly losing weight. No matter how often I nursed him, he would throw it all up. The pediatrician told me it was probably just reflux.

By the time my baby was a month old, I knew it wasn't just reflux. My son was still unable to keep anything down, and he was crying all the time. I rushed back to the pediatrician. This time, he ran tests and found the real cause: a blockage in my son's stomach. I'll never forget when he came into the exam room and told me that my baby needed emergency surgery. The guilt weighing me down became even heavier when the pediatrician added, "Well, now we know why he's been crying so much. He's hungry."

As I buckled my son into his car seat, I began sobbing uncontrollably. The surgery was scheduled for the next morning, and the pediatrician's words rang in my ears: "He's hungry." My son was starving, and it was all my fault. Or so I told myself. After all, I had to get everything right, all the time.

The surgery was a success. Over the next couple of days, I pumped my breast milk at the hospital so we could adequately measure his intake through bottle-feeding. In the process of taking the bottle, he decided he was done with nursing, which further complicated my guilt. Today, I see the whole situation through a much clearer lens, but at the time, I felt like I had failed my child.

When we believe the lie that we can't get anything wrong, we can develop a guilt complex. *Guilt complex* can be defined as "a persistent belief that you have done something wrong or that you will do something wrong."³ While this complex can be the result of actual wrongdoing (true guilt), it can also emerge from perceived guilt (false guilt) over something outside your control.

If you have a guilt complex, you tend to feel guilt even in situations when you have done nothing wrong or perhaps overthink your role in a situation and conclude that your actions or inactions played a much bigger part than they actually did. A guilt complex can take over when we aren't aware of what unconnected factors may be causing us to amplify the feeling that we've done something wrong—and many of us come into parenting with a guilt complex fully established:

- **Anxiety.** If you have a great deal of anxiety, you may be more likely to negatively assess your own actions in ways that lead to feelings of guilt.

- **Childhood experiences.** Children who are raised in households where they are made to feel that they have done something wrong, have something to hide, or are responsible for problems may be left with lingering feelings of guilt.

- **Culture.** If you find yourself doing things that are in opposition to the cultural norms you were raised with, you may experience guilt even if you no longer believe in or support those norms.

- **Religion.** Some religious traditions rely on feelings of guilt as a way to indicate that a person has done something wrong.

- **Social pressure.** If you feel that other people are judging you for the things that you have done, you may be left with feelings of guilt and remorse.[4]

These hidden contributing factors explain my tendency to live with a cloud of low-level guilt that causes me to second-guess and overestimate my role in innocuous situations. And when I have legitimately done something wrong, they can cause the guilt to run wild, still eating me alive long after I've taken action to remedy the situation. Maybe you can relate.

The good news is that God didn't create us to live with a guilt complex. He sees the crushing effects of guilt and shame, and he offers a solution to set us free.

> God did not send his Son into the world to condemn the world, but to save the world through him. Whoever believes in him is not condemned, but whoever does not believe stands condemned already because they have not believed in the name of God's one and only Son.
> JOHN 3:17-18

> "Very truly I tell you, whoever hears my word and believes him who sent me has eternal life and will not be judged but has crossed over from death to life."
> JOHN 5:24

Grace, without fail, always extinguishes guilt. God sent his Son to pay the penalty for our sins and lift the heavy burden of guilt and shame. We are no longer under condemnation. His redemptive plan isn't simply a practical exchange where Jesus pays the penalty, we acknowledge the sacrifice, and while we receive the benefit of forgiveness and eternal life, we're left to deal with ongoing guilt and shame. Instead, all the way back in the Garden of Eden, God began showing us that guilt and shame aren't what he wants for us. When Adam and Eve sinned, not only did he forgive them, he went a step further—he made "garments of skin" for them, clothing them to cover their shame and guilt (Genesis 3:21). He did the same thing to a much greater degree on the cross, not just covering our sin with the sacrifice of his Son but going a step further in offering freedom from guilt and shame.

Knowing this about God, how do you think he feels about the false guilt we carry as mothers? Even if we're feeling guilty about an actual wrongdoing, we're not meant to live in it; guilt is a nudge in our conscience, a conviction when we do wrong, so we might respond with a godly sorrow that leads to repentance (see 2 Corinthians 7:10). In those instances, guilt is a tool, not a sentence. Once we repent, we leave that guilt behind us forever. God has forgiven us, and when he looks at us, he sees the righteousness of Christ. God does not declare us guilty, so we shouldn't declare ourselves guilty either.

If God doesn't want you to carry a burden of guilt even in situations of true guilt, why then would he want you to carry any false guilt? And hear me on this: Most motherhood guilt falls into the category of false guilt, which is rooted in a failure to perform up to an impossible standard of perfection. The guilt you feel is not of God or from God.

The only way to live in the freedom of being a good-enough mom is to adopt the same attitude about guilt that God has. God wants us to trade our *guilt complex* for a *grace complex*.

As I was writing this chapter, I asked mothers to share about the last time they experienced motherhood guilt. You'll probably recognize yourself in some of their answers. But I want us to move beyond just naming the guilt. What would it look like if we traded it for grace?

> "I don't play enough with my children or spend enough one-on-one time with them."

- **Guilt Complex:** *I am shortchanging my children by not playing with them more. They don't feel as loved or valuable as they should because I can't spend as much time with them as I know I should. My failure to play with my children enough may even impact them on some level in the future.*

- **Grace Complex:** *I am doing the best job I can to care for myself and my family given the current situation and my capacity. My sanity and self-care are important. Sometimes I am too busy or exhausted to play and I need a break. Occasionally saying no to my children helps them learn to entertain themselves and stimulate their imaginations and creativity. God has extended his grace to me, and therefore I will extend that same grace to myself.*

"I work outside the home and should invest in my kids and home as much as I can when I am present."

- **Guilt Complex:** *Since I work, I owe my children my undivided attention while we are home together. When I don't measure up to that standard, I feel like I am letting them down. They deserve a mother who can give them more attention.*

- **Grace Complex:** *Whether I am working due to financial necessity or personal preference, I am not doing anything wrong by working. Children are resilient and can adapt to this rhythm. Some days or weeks will be harder than others, and this is an opportunity to work together as a family and grow closer. My children are more likely to remember the quality of the time we spend together than the quantity, so I will relieve myself of the pressure to spend every spare moment with them. God has extended his grace to me, and therefore I will extend that same grace to myself.*

"I should be spending quality time with each child, volunteering at their schools, and attending every single one of their activities and events."

- **Guilt Complex:** *Other moms seem to get more done than me. They seem to have more time, energy, resources, and creativity to do it all. I feel like I am failing my children when I can't perform at the same level.*

- **Grace Complex:** *The assumption that mothers can do it all is a bold-faced lie. I will no longer subject myself to this ridiculous standard of perfection that is impossible to achieve. I am the exact mother God assigned to my children, and I am letting myself off the hook to be anyone other than myself. God has extended his grace to me, and therefore I will extend that same grace to myself.*

Do you notice the *should*s and *enough*s in these kinds of guilt complexes? Those are a signal of an undefined guilt—because *should* and *enough* are limitless, impossible to measure or reach.

We have to learn to tell ourselves a different story when it comes to guilt. We must resist the notion that guilt is a standard part of the motherhood package. This was never God's intent or desire, and to believe it was is to believe a lie.

What, then, is the truth?

> This is how we know that we belong to the truth and how we set our hearts at rest in his presence: If our hearts condemn us, we know that God is greater than our hearts, and he knows everything.
> 1 JOHN 3:19-20

Various words used in the Bible could refer to the heart. This particular passage speaks of the heart three times, each time using the word *kardia*. *Kardia* can refer to the center of a person's thoughts and feelings.[5]

Try reading the passage below from your perspective with the broader Greek meaning inserted:

> This is how I know that I belong to the truth and how I set my *thoughts and feelings* at rest in his presence: If my *thoughts and feelings* condemn me, I know that God is greater than my *thoughts and feelings*, and he knows everything.

God's Word is so powerful. He literally lays out a strategy to help us extinguish guilt and shame. If you struggle with motherhood guilt (or guilt of any kind), I encourage you to memorize the passage above in first person. Say it out loud and declare God's truth. God is greater than our thoughts and feelings.

We develop a grace complex over time as we grow in our relationships with Christ and spend time in his Word. The more we become steeped in his truth, the less likely we are to fall for the familiar guilt traps. Guilt is nothing more than a thought or a feeling. It does not have the ability to exert power over our lives unless we choose to give it power. The next time you find yourself feeling guilt, rely on God's power and proclaim his truth.

THE FREEDOM OF *GOOD ENOUGH*

One of the greatest blessings in my life has been working with refugees, most of whom have fled their homelands due to persecution or the constant threat of danger. I have grown close to some of the mothers in the community, and they have given me a different perspective on motherhood.

Years ago, I helped set up a small apartment for a refugee family who was arriving in the United States after years of waiting for approval in a refugee camp. I knew they had an infant, so I gathered up baby gadgets to help ease their transition. When I stopped by to check on them a few weeks in, the baby gadgets were piled on the baby bed, still unused. The mother had no need of a baby swing, bouncer seat, high chair, or stroller. She wore her baby most of the day and laid her baby down on the bed to nap. In her culture, families co-sleep when the children are young, likely because they don't have the luxury of separate bedrooms, much less beds. All the gadgets were just taking up much-needed space.

The reality is that motherhood looks different for my friends for a lot of reasons, some of which are very difficult. Most live below the poverty line and have limited resources. Often they don't speak the majority-culture language. Many have experienced trauma. My refugee friends don't feel the burdensome weight of "good mother" expectations because fulfilling them isn't an option. When getting by day-to-day is the top priority, there's not a whole lot of space for agonizing over missed parent-teacher conferences or forgotten school lunches or homework assignments.

But what amazes me most when I observe their culture is that despite these struggles these mothers seem to have less stress and more joy. And without the white noise of constant activity and a proliferation of stuff, most of their children are thriving. Because they often don't have internet, they don't spend too much time on their tablets. Their social life typically centers around their community and church. They teach themselves or each other to drive because they can't afford a formal driver's ed course, and they work hard to save up for a used vehicle or share a vehicle with other family members. Many of the older children go on to attend community college, work part-time or full-time jobs to help with the bills, and tend to their younger siblings. They are respectful to their parents and deeply grateful for the sacrifices their parents have made to give them better lives.

My refugee friends show me what living in grace looks like. They are not burdened by guilt, because they understand and accept their limitations. They rest content in *good enough*.

You can experience the same freedom. Guilt is debilitating. Crushing. Wearisome. Exhausting. You can decide right now that you are going to let yourself off the hook to have it all together. To get it all right. To be perfect.

Can you imagine what a difference that kind of freedom would make in your life? Your parenting? Your overall well-being?

You deserve to be free. Your first step is accepting that you are already good enough. It's time to cancel the guilt trip and live in grace.

REFLECTION QUESTIONS

1. Consider a recent guilt trip you experienced as a mother. Do you think it was true guilt or false guilt? Why?

2. List some of the "good mother" lies you've fallen for, and then take some time to refute each one with the truth.

3. Are you more prone to a guilt complex or a grace complex? If you are more prone to guilt, why do you think that is? What steps might you take to adopt more of a grace complex?

4. How might finding freedom in *good enough* impact the guilt you carry in motherhood?

THREE

GOOD FOR HER, NOT FOR ME

The Grace of Acceptance

Let us therefore make every effort to do what
leads to peace and to mutual edification.
ROMANS 14:19

It was my oldest child's first official swim lesson. He was four years old, and I had secured him a spot with a well-known swim teacher who had been teaching kids to swim in her backyard pool for a dozen or more years. During the lesson, I chatted with a few of the other moms who sat in a waiting area on the patio. When the first lesson concluded, I began to round up my son's things and asked him to grab his towel.

As he went to fetch it, the swim teacher turned to me and said in a scolding tone, "What is it with you younger mothers always asking your children to do what should naturally be expected of them? It is not your child's choice to decide. You tell them—you don't ask them!"

My face immediately flushed with embarrassment over the public chastisement. As I nudged my son to comply, wanting to make a speedy exit out the back gate, one of the other moms shot me a compassionate glance of support. While that small kindness may have taken the edge off in the moment, the sting of the teacher's words left me feeling as if I'd intentionally done something wrong.

If there's a universal motherhood experience, it's the judgment of those who think they know better. But while my generation of mothers certainly faced the occasional sideways glance or stinging remark, we didn't carry the weight of the watching world the way moms do today. Parenting advice was limited to the books and magazines we read, our immediate peer group of fellow mothers, our own mothers and mentors, the church, and our pediatricians. We gravitated to like-minded mothers who offered a smaller, more intimate support network and helped reduce the loneliness of motherhood. If we needed guidance or advice, our trusted advisors were usually a phone call or front-porch visit away. We were picky about whom we let into our world and had the luxury of deciding whom we trusted for advice when challenges arose.

But thanks to social media, motherhood today has become a spectator sport. Mothers are exposed to a constant drip of online advice and a steady stream of perfectly curated images and highlight reels depicting the highs and lows of motherhood. (Mainly the highs.) Social media offers a sneak peek into the lives of mothers far and wide—friend, foe, family member, celebrity, or mere stranger. This phenomenon has created a whole new level of expectations—an ever-present, ever-shifting measure of exceptional motherhood that can serve as a source of external judgment from people posturing as motherhood know-it-alls and a quieter, *how-do-I-measure-up?* internal judgment. Technology has given everyone a platform and a megaphone to weigh in. Welcome to the vortex of motherhood madness, where anyone can become an armchair parenting expert.

In addition to the online pressures related to motherhood, there are the cultural pressures. Whether the buzzworthy topic is natural birth versus medicated birth, breastfeeding versus bottle-feeding, homeschool versus private school versus public school, being a work-outside-the-home mom versus being a work-in-the-home mom, vaccine theories, discipline philosophies, sex education, nutrition advice, screen guidelines for children, mental-health concerns, or something else, there is no shortage of opinions. And those opinions usually come with judgment attached. No matter where you line up on the spectrum of issues, there will be plenty of detractors waiting in the wings to call you out and leave you second-guessing your position.

And then there are the expectations placed on mothers by the Christian community, our churches, and fellow Christian mothers. While we've seen a lot of progress in how mothers and fathers share in the management and upbringing of children in recent decades, many faith communities still view the mother as the primary caregiver even if both parents work full-time jobs. Christian mothers are bombarded with strong opinions related to marriage and parenthood, often backed up with an out-of-context Bible verse or two. Some messages are particularly dangerous because they condition Christian mothers to mask or ignore their own needs and mental health for the sake of serving their husbands and children.

"Lose the baby weight," "Dress attractively," "Keep a tidy house," "Don't decline your husband's sexual advances," and other unrealistic marriage expectations are often added to the giant heap of motherhood expectations moms already carry.

The constant onslaught of expectations can create an environment where motherhood seems more like a competition than a sisterhood. It becomes a contest of sorts, where mothers of all ages and stages are pitted against one another to prove they've got it right (or at least mostly right).

When we discussed the difference between true guilt and false guilt in the previous chapter, we learned that judgment is a key contributing factor to both. Like guilt, judgment is not always a bad thing. Judgment allows us to weigh options and make necessary assessments on a daily basis. But that type of healthy judgment—maybe better called *discernment*—can morph into contempt for other perspectives or positions should they not match our own. It is this brand of judgment that is toxic to motherhood.

Even sadder, this brand of toxic judgment robs us of relationship and connection with others. Rather than bond with other mothers over the shared sentiment that motherhood is hard and often rife with unreasonable expectations, we create a culture where we are wary of one another. Motherhood is not a competition; it is a team sport. And when we don't have a team, it can feel very isolating and lonely.

CONNECTION OVER COMPARISON

Back when I was a mother of littles in the pre-internet, pre-smartphone late 1980s and early 1990s, my go-to escape was usually a quick phone call with a fellow mom friend to help break up the chaos of the day. With our brick-sized cordless phone wedged between our ear and shoulder, we learned to master the art of folding laundry, cooking dinner, breaking up sibling fights, and doing other daily chores with a friend in our ear. Some days, we'd talk so long the battery would run down and our phones would beep at us until we returned them to their bases for a recharge. Those phone conversations, alongside mothers' groups, Bible studies, and church socials, were a lifeline in my early motherhood days, reminding me that I was not alone.

These days, many moms look to social media for support and encouragement. Social media offers a means to document your own motherhood memories, stay up to date with friends, or "follow" other moms you respect from afar. Whether you are feeling confused, overwhelmed, underappreciated, or annoyed with your kids (or husband), you are only a hashtag away from the largest virtual support group on the planet, offering camaraderie accessible around the clock, twenty-four seven. You can even weigh in by contributing to the 84.8 million (and counting) posts related to #momlife. The instant connection with moms can help reduce the aloneness many moms experience in the daily grind of motherhood.

The upside of this instant—and distant—connection is unfortunately also the downside. Because absent of real relationship and trust, the instant and distant motherhood connections online can very quickly lead us into that destructive form of judgment brought on by comparison.

Now, when it comes to the pressures of comparison and judgment on social media, I want to acknowledge that this is not a one-size-fits-all issue. Everyone is different, and some mothers are more adversely affected than others. The key will be determining where you fall on the scale.

Comparing ourselves to others is natural and was even recognized as a legitimate behavioral theory in 1954 by psychologist Leon Festinger. Social comparison theory, as it's known, is "the idea that individuals determine their own social and personal worth based on how they stack up against others."[1] Some studies suggest "as much as 10 percent of our thoughts involve comparisons of some kind."[2] We vacillate between upward social comparison and downward social comparison. In upward comparisons, we evaluate ourselves next to those we believe are "better than" us (in performance, appearance, etc.). In downward comparisons, we compare ourselves to those we believe *we* are "better than." The first is judgment of ourselves; the second is judgment of others (and, often, how we experience judgment *from* others).

I should note that social comparison is not always a bad thing. In many cases, it can cause us to assess areas of weakness and serve as a motivator to improve. However, it can also have the reverse effect, especially if we are looking to a context disconnected from embodied relationship as a constant source of comparison. Whether you're encountering a snippet of news related to a celebrity who seems to have it all together on the motherhood front, a fellow mom in your book club who never seems tired or worn down by her children, or a public speaker at a women's event who offers performative-based formulas for motherhood, it's hard not to find yourself engaged in a comparison trap.

Social media gives mothers the opportunity to curate their own brand of motherhood—complete with carefully chosen pictures and content—and rarely do we know what is really going on behind the edited scenes of a person's life. This is especially true if it involves someone who is not an actual acquaintance or friend. When we aren't in real-life, day-to-day connection with people, what we see is not always a true picture of reality.

Likewise, when we post, we can choose the snapshots of our lives we want others to see. Measuring ourselves against a highlight reel can take a mental toll on our souls if we have a habit of engaging in upward social comparison and are regularly reminded that our current reality doesn't match what we see from others—or even what we'd like others to see from us.

One reason we are attracted to influencers is the idealistic fantasy that someone has cracked the code when it comes to living a fulfilling life. The word *idealistic* offers some valuable insight when it comes to our innate desire to engage in upward social comparison. *Ideal* in the adjective form means "constituting a standard of perfection or excellence."[3] Mothers are particularly susceptible to this trap because we desperately want to be the best mothers possible to our children (remember the guilt trap!). We long for a get-it-right standard, a formula, a blueprint to achieve the imagined nirvana of "excellence," and we lack a standard litmus test to gauge our progress. No wonder we are drawn to social media, where there is no shortage of mothers leading seemingly ideal lives who are all too happy to show us the way.

But I believe there is another pull to social media that especially appeals to mothers. It can offer us the illusion of connection or community without requiring an actual investment from us. Relationships are hard, and the potential risk for drama, disagreements, or hurt feelings (which comes with the territory of most relationships) can hinder women from wanting to invest in the hard work of building mutual, life-giving friendships.

Social media will never be a replacement for real relationships and community. Social comparison and the judgment that is often embedded in the formula are inescapable. Besides, the risks involved in a real relationship can help detach us from the judgment trap. Sure, we'll still struggle with social comparison and experience judgment (as well as dole it out) from time to time in our real relationships, but we will have incentive to work through the issues because we care about the person on the other side. If judgment is an ongoing pattern with a particular person, it might be worth reevaluating the friendship, but don't give up without an attempt to work through the situation. In a true friendship, "iron sharpens iron" (Proverbs 27:17).

TO EACH HER OWN

In a widely read 1920s parenting guide called *Psychological Care of Infant and Child*, behavioral psychologist John B. Watson counseled mothers to "never hug and kiss [your child], never let them sit in your lap. If you must, kiss them once on the forehead when they say good night. Shake hands with them in the morning."[4] (In other words, treat them as you would a formal business associate.) But Watson's worst advice was probably this: "Put [your child] out in the backyard a large part of the day. Build a fence around the yard so that you are sure no harm can come to it. Do this from the time [the child] is born. . . . If your heart is too tender and you must watch the child, make yourself a peephole so that you can see it without being seen, or use a periscope."[5]

Another vintage parenting guide offered these gems:

- "Don't permit a child to be in the glare of the sun without a hat . . . he is likely to have a sunstroke, which might either at once kill him, or might make him an idiot for the remainder of his life."[6]

- "Don't cram a wet-nurse with food and give her strong ale to drink."[7]

- "Don't allow your child luncheon. If he wants anything to eat between breakfast and dinner let him have a piece of dry bread."[8]

- "Don't hold children's parties. They are one of the great follies of the present age."[9]

- "Don't punish a child too harshly. . . . Small children may be sent to bed without supper or tied in an arm-chair."[10]

I have so many questions. And yet—this kind of stuff was considered expert parenting advice in the past! It certainly begs the question of how much of the parenting advice we've adopted will be outdated—or worse, deemed irresponsible—in the years to come.

Take, for example, how we choose to feed our babies. Whether to breastfeed or not has been a huge source of guilt for mothers of nearly every generation. In the 1960s, formula was considered superior to breast milk—so much so that when my mother-in-law wanted to try breastfeeding, the pediatrician guilted her and refused to give her any information. She had to go to the library and check out books on breastfeeding to learn more about it!

On the other side, the pressure to breastfeed these days can make moms feel like they're failures if they struggle to nurse their babies or if they simply don't want to. There are a lot of loud voices shouting opinions of "Breast is best!" versus "Bottle is best!" Was one generation right and the other wrong? Are we disqualified from being good mothers if we choose not to adopt the mainstream "expert" positions of the day?

Any mom knows this is true: There are a whole lot of "experts" out there telling us the right way to parent, and as a result, we can land in all sorts of places with parenting choices—and find that judgment can creep in about those who make other choices. We can sometimes let our pursuit of good for our kids turn into a rigid posture of *I have to be right about this*, which results in seeing a whole lot of other people's choices as wrong.

I understand the draw to adopt a parenting position or style that seems certain. What mother doesn't want a map of sorts as she traverses the unknown terrain of raising kids? I found an element of security in following certain experts of my day as well as support from a community of mothers who followed the same experts and advice. Some of the advice aged well and stood the test of time, and some did not. In fact, there are several Christian parenting experts of my day who I would not recommend to your generation based on their extreme stances on discipline and a patriarchal position that puts the bulk of the childcare load on the mother. Many mothers in my generation are unlearning some of the positions we once embraced, but we are also able to acknowledge other truths we learned that were beneficial. In other words, whatever parenting advice we followed, it wasn't *all right* and it wasn't *all wrong*.

Just as no generation of parents should be naïve enough to believe they have all the answers, no individual parent has all the answers either. We make the choices that seem right for our unique family situations in alignment with our values and priorities. Parenting requires ongoing flexibility and adaptability because we are raising human beings, and over time, personalities evolve and needs change.

Parenting involves trial and error, and sometimes we don't understand the errors until much later. Every generation will make mistakes. Just as my generation shook our heads at some of the parenting tactics our parents embraced—and likewise, your generation shakes your head at parenting tactics my generation embraced—know, too, that your children will find a few things to shake their heads over when they grow up.

Much healing can occur if we accept that most parents did the best job they could with the information, resources, and advice available at the time. We can extend the same grace to the generation before us that we hope to someday receive from our children's generation. When we do make mistakes, we can own them, apologize, and ask for forgiveness. In doing so, we create a safe environment for our own children to do the same. If relational harm has occurred, we can welcome feedback without taking personal offense and work toward healing and restoration.

I am certainly not suggesting that we accept and endure ongoing toxic behaviors our parents may display. Restoration cannot occur if the other person is an unwilling party. While we are called to forgive others whether they ask for it or not, that forgiveness does not require us to continue in a relationship where abuse is present and ongoing. If this is your situation, know that I understand as someone who has personally experienced this painful dynamic. As devastating as it was at the time, it made me more intentional in creating a safe environment of open communication with my own children.

There is great freedom that comes in knowing that there is no one right way to parent and that God doesn't require perfection from you. You will get some things right and some things wrong. You will make choices that are right for you and wrong for someone else. And likewise, others will make choices that are good for them but not for you.

CREATING A CULTURE OF NONJUDGMENT

Parenting is complicated and nuanced—rarely does it present binary choices, actions, or decisions. Why, then, do we oftentimes cling to this rigid notion of black and white, right and wrong, good and bad, with little (if any) tolerance for positions that land outside our neat and tidy belief system?

Allow me to speculate based on my own personal experience as a recovering legalist. If you're not familiar with the term, *legalism* can be defined as "judging of conduct in terms of adherence to precise laws."[11] Prescribed rules or laws, which emerge from a fundamentally wise intent, can be a good thing. These kinds of boundaries create order, safety, and security. But legalism goes a step further: We place ourself as the correct judge of both the right boundaries—which often involves adding extra and unnecessary requirements to the good intent—and how other people measure up to those boundaries.

- We value God's Word, but we decide that our particular study approach is the best one and that people who approach Scripture differently have a much lower view of it than we do.

- We want our kids to have healthy relationships with the opposite sex, and we set intentional boundaries to facilitate that—but anyone whose boundaries look different is clearly being overly permissive.

When our identity is misdefined and our worth is rooted in how we perform or is contingent on the approval of others rather than who we are in Christ, faulty judgments can show up all over motherhood. I know because I was this mother.

Getting something wrong went to the core of who I was as a person. I liked the certainty of black and white. Anything in between was in the gray area of subjectivity—and very uncomfortable.

When worth is based on performance or what others think of us, there is little wiggle room to get it wrong, because getting it wrong impacts our identity. And we will go to the mat to protect our identity. When we live in a mindset of *I have to get it right to feel as though I have worth and value,* we will always tend toward legalism and judgment—both self-inflicted and toward others. This is another reason it is of vital importance to properly define our identity in Christ and Christ alone.

The apostle Paul had a few things to say about judgment—and better yet, he offered a solution:

> You, then, why do you judge your brother or sister? Or why do you treat them with contempt? For we will all stand before God's judgment seat. It is written:
>
> "'As surely as I live,' says the Lord,
> 'every knee will bow before me;
>   every tongue will acknowledge God.'"
>
> So then, each of us will give an account of ourselves to God.
>
> Therefore let us stop passing judgment on one another.
>
> **ROMANS 14:10-13**

I especially love the *Message* translation of verse 13:

> Forget about deciding what's right for each other. Here's what you need to be concerned about: that you don't get in the way of someone else, making life more difficult than it already is.
>
> **ROMANS 14:13, MSG**

If ever there was a word for mothers, this is it! While Paul wasn't speaking specifically about motherhood judgment, we can trust that the same truth applies. As Christians, we will someday stand before God and give an account of our lives. What will this account consist of? Well, we know it is not for the sake of deciding our salvation—that has already been decided. But I'm willing to bet that neither will we be grilled by God about our beliefs related to breastfeeding, vaccines, how we chose to educate our children, or parenting philosophies in general. He's not going to quiz us about our preferred worship style, our church attendance, our views on evolution, our interpretation of oft-debated passages of Scripture, our political affiliation, and how we voted in each election (or, for that matter, whether we voted at all). There will be no charts depicting the hills we chose to die on and how many people we successfully recruited over the years to die on the same hills.

What we will be accountable for is how we treated others, including our brothers and sisters in Christ.

Judgment is often used as a legal term in the court of law: A defendant awaits a verdict, or judgment. As mothers, we often feel like we are on trial every day—but the reality is that God, in his mercy, has already rendered a judgment toward us. Participating in his culture of nonjudgment is only possible when we decide to be part of the defense team rather than the judge and jury.

Paul reminds us of what truly matters to God. Rather than spend our time and energy debating tertiary issues that have zero significance from a heavenly perspective, why not follow God's model and extend grace?

When our identity is rooted in who we are in Christ (forgiven of our sins and wholly loved by God), we establish our worth and value on the right foundation. We are free to take ownership of mistakes we make along the way because they don't affect our personhood or identity. In other words, we are no less valuable in God's eyes when we make mistakes. Just as we are no more valuable in his eyes when we "get it right." Grace acknowledges that we are accepted whether we get it right or not.

And here's the beauty of it: When we can extend grace toward ourselves, we can also extend it toward others. We can be spacious and supportive of parenting choices that differ from our own. We can live with an unthreatened posture, knowing that someone else's choice isn't a referendum or judgment on our own but rather what's right for them.

We can say with confidence, "Good for her, not for me," and truly mean it.

REFLECTION QUESTIONS

1. What is one way you have felt judged as a mother? What was your response to the judgment?

2. What role does social media play in your need for connection with other mothers? How has it encouraged comparison that often leads to judgment?

3. Do you tend to gravitate toward positions of certainty in parenting? Do you sometimes believe that an opposing view or position is all wrong? How might it help to learn to say, "Good for her, not for me" and leave it at that?

4. How can you be more intentional about creating a culture of nonjudgment?

5. How does an identity properly rooted in Christ help guard against judgment and support self-acceptance?

FOUR

SLOW DOWN AND SHOW UP

The Grace of Being Present

When I am constantly running there is no time for being.
When there is no time for being there is no time for listening.
MADELEINE L'ENGLE

When I was a young mom, I attended a MOPS (Mothers of Preschoolers) meeting where the guest speaker was talking about being engaged with and present for our children. To reinforce the concept, she shared about a time when her then-high-school-aged children were due home from school at any moment. She was grabbing some items at the grocery store and got caught in a long line. She glanced at her watch and realized her kids would arrive home to an empty house unless she bailed on her grocery cart at that moment and raced home to greet them.

I kept waiting for her to share the catch. Did they forget their house key? Was it their first time to ride the bus? Was it raining that day and a long walk from the bus stop to home? (Even so, would they melt in the rain?) Nope, none of the above. She stated that she simply wanted to be waiting for them when they walked through the door, ready with a smile and an after-school snack. She argued that she could always go back to the store and get the items she needed but couldn't get back the moments she missed with her children.

Sadly, the speaker was reinforcing the "good mother" lie that our children are the center of our lives and, as such, we owe it to them to be present for every possible moment of their childhoods, wide-eyed, alert, and ready to serve. As someone who always worked part-time or full-time while raising my children, I felt particularly insulted over the implication that children with working moms get the short end of the stick. And never mind that most teenagers are hardly ecstatic over the idea of their moms greeting them after school each day, peppering them with dozens of questions.

Being present is about much more than showing up physically for our children and logging as many minutes as possible in their presence. It's about more than rushing from one task to another to prove our love. It's about more than savoring every moment we have with them and making each second as memorable as possible. Most importantly, being present is about more than putting our children at the center of our lives and making them the sole beneficiaries of our mindful attention. Healthy presence is about balance:

- balancing being present through time together alongside being present to an honest approach to life,

- balancing being present to developing skills and creating memories alongside being present to offering space and rest, and

- balancing being present to our family's needs alongside being present to ourselves and our own needs.

BALANCE OVER BUSTLE

My oldest two kids were three and one when I felt the first wave of pressure to jump on the extracurricular bandwagon. I was sitting in a small group when another mother shared how her daughter (age four) was on the waitlist for Suzuki violin lessons and mentioned it as a prayer request. She then proceeded to enlighten the group about the proven benefits of learning to play the violin at an early age. I can't recall the benefits in detail, but I'm pretty sure it amounted to early admittance to Harvard and eventually curing cancer and winning a Nobel Peace Prize.

In that moment, I felt panicked—were my poor children treading a pathway to average? It was time to step up my game. And with that, the rat race began: T-ball, soccer, piano, guitar, drama camp, gymnastics, dance class, competitive cheer, football, basketball, baseball—you name it, and we probably tried it.

If only I could go back and have a little chat with my younger self, I would tell her how easy it is for us to believe the lie that busyness—doing everything we can for our families, all the time, endlessly—is the measure of a good mom.

We have been duped by the lie that good motherhood demands a frenzied pace as the norm. On most days, we feel more like a drill sergeant than a mother, barking out orders to accomplish the mission at hand, and the next one, and then the next:

- "Find your shoes and get in the car."
- "I told you to get dressed ten minutes ago!"
- "Could you move any slower?"
- "I don't have time for this!"
- "Move it! We're going to be late."
- "I don't have time for you to buckle your car seat. Let Mommy do it."

Busyness comes with the territory of motherhood, or so we're often told. And in our rush, we never slow down long enough to ponder whether God endorses the ludicrous pace. (Hint: He doesn't!) Unless we take a deeper look at the source and get honest with ourselves about the underlying motives, we will only be treating the symptoms instead of the disease.

I learned this the hard way. Balancing ministry obligations, book deadlines, out-of-town speaking engagements, a marriage, and three kids with various school and extracurricular activities left me running on empty most days. In my book *Rest Assured: A Recovery Plan for Weary Souls*, I described my awareness of the problem in terms often associated with addiction:

> As I reflected on my tendencies, I realized that something deep within my being was compelling me to maintain the breakneck pace. *Something* drove me to fill every brief pause or empty hour with more activities and commitments. I desperately wanted to put my foot on the brakes and exit the fast lane, but I couldn't bring myself to actually stop the frenzy. I

hated the pace, but at the same time, I *needed* it. I *complained* about it in one breath and *bragged* about it in the next. . . .

I spoke about my life as if I had absolutely no control over the crazy pace, as if some invisible drill sergeant dictated my calendar and made sure every spare moment was productive and useful. My recounting of the pace of my life might have sounded like a woeful complaint, but something else was camouflaged underneath: a slight ring of pride. My frenzied, overbooked calendar was becoming the silent proof to others, and to myself, that my life was full and important. Somewhere along the way, busyness had become the barometer for measuring my worth and value. The busier I was, the more I mattered, or at least that's how I felt.[1]

My pursuit to be *enough* in my ministry, in my marriage, and as a mother was too much, and I eventually buckled under the weight of it all. I had believed the lie that a full calendar and constant activity was evidence of a full life, not just for me but for my children as well. Much of my healing came when I realized that my chronic busyness was a *sin problem* rather than a *scheduling problem*. God never intended me to feel burned out, used up, half alive. Lasting change required a new way of thinking and a new approach to living. God, in his loving mercy, gave me a new perspective when it came to the pursuit of enough. He showed me that the lie of a full life can leave you feeling empty.

Don't get me wrong—I am not suggesting that the goal is to experience a life free of busyness. Although the thought may sound nice, *motherhood* and *free of busyness* are not typically used in the same sentence. The reality is, there will be times that are hectic, or even downright chaotic—but those times should be the exception rather than the norm.

Constant hurry robs us of the centered life God invites us into. If we want to be present, we will need to reject the frantic pace and instead fight for balance. We need to slow down enough to notice the state of our souls, to tune in to the deeper needs beneath our children's deeds, to leave space for unhurried moments for our children and ourselves. Pressing pause to be more present isn't easy, but it's worth fighting for.

Jesus was no stranger to a hectic pace, and yet he was present in the moments that mattered most. His mission was "to proclaim good news to the poor," "to proclaim freedom for the prisoners and recovery of sight for the blind, to set the oppressed free, to proclaim the year of the Lord's favor" (Luke 4:18-19), and he had three short years to accomplish that purpose. The clock was ticking.

Yet Jesus never demonstrated stress or panic, and he never exhibited the frenzied pace we see today. While Jesus lived on earth in bodily form, he was fully God *and* fully human, and he had the capacity to suffer burnout and exhaustion just like any other human being. And like us, each day he had to make choices about how he would spend his time.

When I read an account of a single day in his life recorded in Mark 1:21-34, I'm struck by one word that appears four times in the passage (ESV; emphasis added):

- "They went into Capernaum, and *immediately* on the Sabbath he entered the synagogue and was teaching" (verse 21).
- "*Immediately* there was in their synagogue a man with an unclean spirit" (verse 23).
- "*Immediately* he left the synagogue and entered the house of Simon and Andrew, with James and John" (verse 29).
- "Simon's mother-in-law lay ill with a fever, and *immediately* they told him about her" (verse 30).

Immediately describes the urgency many of us feel to rush from one activity to the next, checking off tasks one by one. But even with the constant pressure to hurry from one thing to another, Jesus set a deliberate pace and moved with a deliberate purpose. He was present in the moment rather than distracted and preoccupied with what came next.

The passage in Mark 1 also tells us that Jesus knew how to draw a healthy boundary between his divine assignment and the never-ending demands that pressed in around him. He didn't let the pressures around him drive his schedule; his mission set his agenda. In Mark 1:36-37, we see the disciples telling him that "everyone is looking for you" (ESV). But Jesus resisted the pressure to play the role they had scripted for him (Mark 1:38). He moved on to the next village to fulfill the assignment God had given him for that place at that time. Jesus knew how and when to say no.

Jesus didn't heal every person, perform hundreds of resurrections, or provide food for every hungry crowd. He did only what his Father had asked him to do in each moment. He took the time to look into people's eyes, listen to their stories, tune in to their needs. And he knew when it was time to disengage from the crowds, find solitude, and be present before God. He offers us the same remedy for our anxious souls.

YOU DON'T HAVE TO CHERISH EVERY SINGLE MOMENT

I was scrolling through my Facebook feed recently when a viral post from an empty-nest mom caught my eye:

> There will come a day when there will be no more jerseys to wash, no more equipment to buy, no more practices to pick kids up from or tournaments to attend. There will come a day when your evenings and weekends are wide open. When your place in the bleachers is filled by another. And you will miss all the running and the reminding and the dirty jerseys piled by the washer. You will miss this season you're in right now. This season of busy.[2]

I'm going to be completely honest with you: While I certainly miss certain moments from the active parenting chapter of my life, I do not miss the busyness, the rushing around, one iota. I don't miss the live-in-my-car shuttle service to school, practices, games, sleepovers, and other activities that consumed our lives for over two decades. I don't miss the epic tantrums, meltdowns, and showdowns with strong-willed toddlers. I don't miss the trips to the school to deliver forgotten lunches, cleats, or homework assignments or the last-minute projects that required late-night runs to the store for poster board. I don't miss the back-to-school activities and countless required forms or the end-of-school-year madness that left everyone in the family on edge. And while I loved watching my children participate in their various sports and extracurricular activities, I don't miss the drama that often accompanied said activities or the jam-packed weekends that left little room to catch our breath before another crazy week began. I happen to love my wide-open evenings and weekends and the current season of life I am in—so . . . thanks, but no thanks!

The truth is that your worth as a woman is not found in the number of dirty jerseys you wash, the amount of time spent driving your children to their activities, or your presence in the bleachers when they perform. *You have intrinsic value apart from what you do for your children.* We shouldn't normalize breakneck busyness as a standard to aspire to and turn it into a badge of honor. On days when your responsibilities exceed your capacity and you're hanging on for dear life by a fraying thread, the last thing you need to hear is an older mom saying, "Enjoy the insanity—this is as good as it gets!" Or, even worse, "You are going to miss this!"

I have good news for you: Your life doesn't end when your children leave, nor is there anything wrong with wishing for a calmer pace. The truth is that if I could go back and do motherhood differently, I would fight for a slower speed, fewer extracurricular activities (especially when my children were younger), and more free time. I would be much more particular about what we said yes to, especially if it meant giving up most every weekend (e.g., attending birthday parties for kids you won't remember in a year). In other words, I would dial it down a notch for more breathing room and more margin to be truly present for what matters most.

Yes, there will be parenting moments you cherish. There will be others you won't. There will be seasons you miss . . . and seasons you can't wait to get out of. And that's perfectly normal.

Being present isn't the same as cherishing every moment, documenting every event, or making sure each day is memorable for your children. It's about showing up and tuning in to the moments that matter most. Sometimes it's active listening as your toddler struggles to find the right words. Other times it's bedtime prayers and "one more book." It can be sitting next to your child, watching their favorite TV show, and laughing along with them. It can be playing a board game with your preteen or taking your teen shopping and grabbing their favorite drink along the way. It's tuning in to the cues behind their "bad moods" and helping them unpack their emotions.

It's time to set yourself free from the "good mother" lie that pressures you to cherish every single moment. Being present doesn't require you to pretend to love it all. True presence is authentic and honest. And *that's* worth cherishing.

GUARDING AGAINST DISTRACTIONS

A mother can take only so much sibling rivalry, extracurricular exhaustion, and homework battling—never mind the sheer pressure of the motherhood lie that mothers should be present and available to their children twenty-four seven without needing a diversion or a means of escape. Whether it's bingeing Netflix, escaping into podcasts, playing games on your phone, watching Hallmark movies, filling up an Amazon cart, or heading to Target, there are plenty of ways to get a break.

There is nothing wrong with engaging in mindless breaks from time to time. The problem comes when these distractions become your preference or your default escape. Take social media, for instance. Social media offers a one-stop shop for moms in need of a mindless few minutes. In fact, you don't even have to know what you are looking for—the algorithm knows you better than you know yourself! Remodeling your kitchen? Need baby-name ideas? Looking for the perfect shade of white paint? Recipes for the Thanksgiving gathering? It's all just a tap away.

It shouldn't come as a surprise that many mothers escape to social media. But social-media platforms were intentionally designed to be addictive. Adam Alter, psychologist and professor of marketing at New York University's Stern School of Business, says social-media sites like Instagram are addictive because "unlike a magazine, television show, or video game, the platform rarely delivers 'stopping cues'—or gentle nudges that prompt users to move on to a different activity."[3] And without stopping cues, it's easy for *distracted and disengaged* to become the norm and rob us of the ability to be *present and engaged* to those who matter most.

When I think about our susceptibility to distractions that hinder us from practicing presence, I'm reminded of the biblical narrative about two sisters, Mary and Martha. The Scripture passage tells us Martha was frustrated because Mary left her alone to deal with the dinner preparations for their very important houseguest, Jesus. Mary "sat at the Lord's feet and listened to his teaching" while Martha was "distracted with much serving" (Luke 10:39-40, ESV). The Greek word translated "distracted" in this passage is *perispaō*, which can mean "to drag all around."[4]

What drags you all around on your average day? What distracts you from practicing the type of presence Mary exhibited—an attentive, intentional posture of tuning in to the moment at hand?

Fortunately, the story doesn't end there. Martha, in her frustration to get the meal on the table, appeals to Jesus to tell her sister to give her a hand. Jesus' response likely caught her off guard.

> Martha was distracted with much serving. . . .
> "Martha, Martha, you are anxious and troubled about many things, but one thing is necessary. Mary has chosen the good portion, which will not be taken away from her."
> LUKE 10:40-42, ESV

Basically, Jesus was saying, "Girl, chill! It's too much!" Jesus loved Martha enough to offer her insight into the root of her problem. One Bible commentary notes that in repeating her name "he speaks as one in earnest, and deeply concerned for her welfare. Those that are entangled in the cares of this life are not easily disentangled."[5] Jesus knew that unless Martha acknowledged the real distraction that hindered her from sitting at his feet and being present in the moment, her pattern would continue. Being present is about discerning what's most important and making the best choice in the given situation.

Jesus wasn't condemning Martha's act of serving but rather making a statement about how "much serving" was dragging her around. The key word here is *much* (the Greek word *polys*).[6] One Bible commentary says, "Some expositors have taken the expression to mean 'a single dish is sufficient' for my entertainment."[7] Another commentary notes, "Whereas Martha was in care to provide many dishes of meat, there was occasion but for one, one would be enough."[8] It seems that Martha's striving to provide an exceptional meal caused her to miss a truly exceptional experience: being present in an important moment with Jesus.

DETERMINING THE NECESSARY

Most mothers share a common desire: We want to offer our children a happy and well-adjusted childhood. To do that, healthy presence is key. If staying present means being intentional about what we don't do, it also means keeping our focus on what we should do.

Philosopher Henry David Thoreau once said, "When the mathematician would solve a difficult problem, he first frees the equation of all incumbrances, and reduces it to its simplest terms. So simplify the problem of life, distinguish the necessary and the real."⁹ What is necessary in your life? What is real?

If we are to distinguish between "the necessary" and "the real," we have to face the world's lie that good mothers expose their children to every activity under the sun. I understand the pressure you are under. Not only have I heard the justifications—I've also said them:

- "How will my children know what their gifts are unless I introduce them to a variety of activities?"
- "I want them to become well-rounded adults."
- "It's competitive out there, and a padded résumé may set my kids apart from other college applicants."
- "I like to keep them busy so they don't have time to get into trouble."

Yes, not all forms of busyness are unhealthy. Not all well-filled calendars are toxic. Many people experience bouts of seasonal busyness that are exceptions to an otherwise well-balanced pace of life. But we are forgetting to consider what's actually necessary when a season of frenzy has given way to a lifestyle of chaos.

Many mothers set forth with pure intentions, believing busyness is the best path to success. We engage our children in activities that will help them tap into their gifts and discover their callings. We want them to have life experiences that will contribute to their educational, emotional, physical, and spiritual well-being. We make countless sacrifices to offer our kids a better world than we had growing up.

God bless my firstborn child, who was raised by two firstborns. (We've jokingly offered to cover any therapy costs he may need as a result of this unfortunate firstborn trifecta.) When he was four, we signed him up for a soccer league despite the reality that he showed zero interest in kicking the ball around in our backyard. Of course, we ended up with a weekly scheduled sideline meltdown and a determined refusal to play—*every single game* . . . even when bribed with that exciting 1990s currency, a McDonald's Happy Meal afterward. (On the upside, I didn't have to wash his jersey the entire season, and it was dirt- and grass-stain free for the end-of-season team picture.)

This is the same firstborn child who got a blowout pirate-themed five-year-old birthday party complete with a treasure map for each guest that led them through a maze of challenges in our backyard and culminated in the playscape gravel pit with spray-painted *X*s to indicate where I'd buried the treasure. I also rented a Captain Hook costume for my husband and told him to chase the children around the backyard as they hunted for their buried treasure. (The more introverted children in the bunch are probably still in counseling over this.) Later, as we were circling the kids up for a game of musical chairs on the driveway, I noticed that the birthday boy was nowhere to be seen. I finally found him inside, sitting quietly in the living room, putting together a LEGO model he'd received as a gift. When I asked him if he wanted to come outside and play party games, he simply replied, "No. I'm ready for my friends to go home now."

In my desire to offer my son "much," I missed the mark on what he would have considered *just enough*—a calmer, quieter birthday celebration with a handful of family and friends. If I had it to do over, I'd save my money, my time, and my sanity.

I am certainly not suggesting that fun birthday parties and extracurricular activities are a waste of time. My husband and I loved cheering our children on in their various pursuits. When properly balanced, these activities can help children develop team-building skills and aid in their overall maturity. But balance is the key. If these activities dominate the calendar and leave us little room to breathe, they become counterproductive and can yield more exhaustion than enrichment.

You have only so much time in a day. It is easy to get caught up in the trap of believing that every spare moment should be invested in your children. You can support your kids in their various activities without sacrificing your own sanity. When we base choices on what's necessary for our families' real needs, we are able to be more present in the moments that matter most.

LEARNING TO BE STILL

One of the assignments God has given you is to raise your children. But he's never expected you to lose yourself in the process. Often we associate the act of staying present as something mothers do for their children, but it's every bit as important to stay present to yourself and your own needs. Besides, what benefit are you to your children if the pursuit to be present in their lives leaves you coming up empty in your own?

Somewhere along the way, we absorbed the lie that mothers should always come last. (We'll dive deeper into self-care in the final chapter.) Learning to be present to ourselves helps set the stage for loving and caring for ourselves.

Being present in your life involves paying attention to your surroundings, engaging your senses to notice the things around you that often get overlooked. When was the last time you paused to listen to the sound of rain falling? Or watch a lightning storm light up the sky? When was the last time you tuned in to the birds chirping in the early morning, signaling the start of a new day? Or went on a walk and picked wildflowers for yourself? Being present means embracing silence and checking in with yourself emotionally. It is taking the time to sit with unpleasant thoughts and feelings to gain a better understanding of yourself.

Tuning in to ourselves and our needs is not selfish. It is a necessity. Becoming more personally present requires the intentional practice of self-awareness—physically, mentally, emotionally, and spiritually. Oftentimes we miss the blessing of being present in our own lives because we struggle to live in the here and now. We allow our minds to wander with thoughts of what has been or what needs to be done, even though the past has already passed and the future has yet to come. Being present to ourselves is focusing on the here and now. What's on your mind *now*? How are you feeling *now*? What's on your heart *now*? What is your body telling you *now*? What are your surroundings *now*? What might you be missing by failing to reflect on the *here and now*?

Being present is fully engaging in the moment and

resisting the common escapes that rob you of the ability to assess your own thoughts, feelings, and needs. Awareness isn't possible without solitude and stillness. Reflection doesn't occur in the hurried rush of life.

Pastor and writer Henri Nouwen calls solitude "the furnace of transformation." He goes on to say,

> In solitude I get rid of my scaffolding: no friends to talk with, no telephone calls to make, no meetings to attend, no music to entertain, no books to distract, just me—naked, vulnerable, weak, sinful, deprived, broken—nothing. It is this nothingness that I have to face in my solitude, a nothingness so dreadful that everything in me wants to run to my friends, my work, and my distractions so that I can forget my nothingness and make myself believe that I am worth something.[10]

Hear me out—unless disconnection is the norm, your children will not suffer long-term damage if you need to take space for solitude. If you have practiced a rhythm of slowing down and being present in their lives, this is what they will remember as the norm. In fact, it is healthy for children to understand that mothers also have needs—and that sometimes they need to take a break. There will be times in your children's lives when you simply don't have the capacity to show up fully (mentally, emotionally, physically). Maybe it's an illness, a time of grief, a struggle with your mental health, or a work project with an urgent deadline. These things are inevitable. If your child sprained their ankle, would you demand they toss the crutches and walk at the same pace during their recovery as they did prior to the injury? Of course not! Sometimes, it's necessary to extend the same grace and compassion to ourselves that we would to our children.

When I think about what it means to be present in our own lives, I am reminded of Psalm 46:10: "Be still, and know that I am God." Some Bible translations use "cease striving" in place of "be still,"[11] which is a bit more descriptive. God calls us to cease striving to be perfect. Cease striving to gain the approval of others. Cease striving to go overboard on tasks that won't matter a year from now. Cease striving to be someone you're not. Cease striving to add more to your to-do list when God calls you to slow down and rest. Cease striving to meet the needs of everyone but yourself.

The problem is, many of us see God as more of a taskmaster than a loving Father. And who among us wants to show up and be still in his presence if we think we're about to get a lecture on how to be a better mom—or a better Christian, for that matter? Often, our misunderstanding of who God is, and likewise who we are to God, hinders us from wanting to slow down and show up . . . not only to God but also to ourselves and others. Experiencing the grace of being present begins with tapping into the grace of God. He is our filling station. In the silence, stillness, and solitude at his feet, we are reminded of our identity in him. God longs for our company and presence. And *that* is worth slowing down for.

REFLECTION QUESTIONS

1. How do you feel about your current pace, and more importantly, the impact it has on your ability to be present?

2. Do you feel pressured to cherish every moment with your children? What would it look like for you to be set free from that motherhood lie?

3. Are you more of a Mary or a Martha? What commonly distracts you or "drags you all around," hindering you from being present in the moments that matter most?

4. What steps can you take to reduce your load and focus on what is necessary?

5. Is being still before God difficult for you? Why or why not?

FIVE

WORRY DOESN'T GET TO RUN THE SHOW

The Grace of Releasing What If . . . ?

[Jesus said,] "Peace I leave with you; my peace I give you. I do not give to you as the world gives. Do not let your hearts be troubled and do not be afraid."
JOHN 14:27

As I changed my first baby out of his hospital-issued baby gown and into the cotton romper I'd purchased as his going-home outfit, I suddenly found myself overwhelmed by how tiny and fragile he was. Sure, he was over eight and a half pounds, but the closest I'd come to dressing anything this small was probably a doll in my childhood years. This was a living, breathing, tiny, helpless human. My husband and I were so young, so inexperienced. And *we were in charge of keeping this baby safe.* When the nurse came in with our discharge papers, I half expected her to intervene and call a halt to the whole shebang. Instead, she went over circumcision and umbilical-cord care, breastfeeding tips to get him to latch properly, and other basics. A few signatures later, we were walking out the hospital doors. I had never been much of a worrier before, but worry decided to take up residence in my life along with this baby.

Worry didn't leave when our daughter was born and we felt a bit more qualified. It stuck around when her younger brother came along and we were seasoned pros. In fact, the list of things to worry about seemed to grow longer over the years:

- fevers, ear infections, and rashes with no explanation . . .
- tumbles meriting stitches, splints, or casts . . .
- academic challenges, hurt feelings, rejections, and heartbreaks . . .
- dangers lurking online, bullying, and standard teenage mental-health concerns . . .
- missed curfews, questionable friendships, teenage angst, peer pressure, and outright rebellion . . .
- driving risks, unchaperoned parties, college-entrance exams . . .
- ultimately, their respective flights out of the nest

It's impossible not to worry about your kids. Parenthood is full of unexpected anxieties and hold-your-breath moments when you have no choice but to trust and pray. And if you assume that motherhood worries will evaporate like the morning dew the day after your last child flies the nest . . . I hate to burst your bubble. You swap old worries for new ones—and as a bonus, you take on a few more when grandkids arrive.

If motherhood worry has an upside, it is evidence that we love our children deeply and want the best for them. Much of our worry is rooted in a desire for our children to have safe, happy, and healthy lives. We don't want them to struggle. We don't want them to suffer. We don't want them to experience unpleasantness.

And in the right dose, worry can be a good thing. It can alert our bodies to potential danger and propel us to move ourselves and our kids to safety. Worry can also force us to examine a situation and consider potential outcomes, helping us develop a course of action toward a good solution. From a spiritual perspective, worry can remind us that a loving, omnipotent God is in control and can be trusted—that faith always eclipses fear.

But as all of us know, worry can quickly become excessive, sending fear signals that are out of sync with the situation, emerging in patterns of anxious thoughts and hypervigilance. It's important to note that worry is different from chronic anxiety, which has a strong chemical component. It is never a sin to struggle with anxiety or to seek counseling or medical help. In fact, it is an act of courage to take the necessary steps to address the problem and find relief. Worry, in contrast, is a choice rooted in what we dwell on and how we respond to what we encounter. Whereas anxiety is more pervasive and produces physical symptoms, worry tends to be situation specific and more of a mental process.

Worry is nothing more than an emotional response, and it can be a signal or a shackle—a temporary visitor or a longtime guest. It can serve a purpose, or it can become an anchor in our souls. It doesn't have the power to control our lives unless we grant it permission to do so.

The good news is that we can opt out of the "good mother" lie that we must be aware of and attentive to every threat or unpleasantness our children may possibly encounter. With practice, we can learn to put worry in its proper place.

A WORLD OF WORRY

I used to be chill. That's what I discovered as my husband and I were watching some old home videos of our children, occasionally wincing and wondering out loud what we could have been thinking. In one clip, my kids were trying out a newly installed zip line in the tree house my husband had built. I held my breath as I watched my three-year-old son (yes, *three*!) stand at the opening of the upper level of the tree house, reach for the zip line handle—and then hang on for dear life as he whooshed from his perch nine feet up and thirty feet toward his father, who waited to catch him at the end. Then there was the video of our children sliding down the stairs headfirst on cardboard panels. Or the one where our sons took turns going down our long, sloping driveway on an old rolling office chair they'd found in the garage, aiming to crash into a pile of cushions.

As I watched these scenes play out, I found myself wondering who that mother was, laughing softly as she filmed her children's daredevil acts. I hardly recognized her. I couldn't imagine allowing my young grandchildren to zip-line from the upper level of a tree house or roll down a steep driveway on an office chair! At what point did I transition from a chill mom to an overprotective Mimi who murmurs "Be careful" on repeat when the grands are in my care? When did the fear set in—and more importantly, why?

The norms in my own childhood help explain my early days of laid-back mothering. There were no car-seat or seatbelt laws, outlet protectors, or guidelines for the safest way to put a baby to sleep. Our parents swaddled us in blankets, surrounded us with plush toys, and laid us in whatever position guaranteed the greatest odds of us sleeping through the night. There were no baby monitors or baby gates. We kids stood up in the back seats of our cars or fought with our siblings over who could sleep on the back-seat ledge under the windshield on family vacations. We were taught a few simple stranger-danger rules, which amounted to "Never answer the door for strangers" and "Never disclose that your parents aren't home" when answering the landline phone.

Many of us walked home alone from elementary school, let ourselves in with a house key, and were on our own until our parents got home from work. In the summer, we played outside with neighbor kids until the streetlights came on at dusk. Our babysitters were barely old enough to not need a sitter themselves. As teens, we drove the moment we turned sixteen, sooner if we could get approved for a "hardship license," which was common for kids with working parents. We hopped on freeways to get places, navigating with fold-up maps that we barely knew how to decipher. If we got lost, we pulled over and asked store clerks for directions. If we weren't going to make curfew, we had to find a pay phone to call our parents, or we didn't call at all. And I don't recall my mother, or other mothers in her generation of mothers, worrying all that much.

When I asked some mom friends my age what they worried about when raising their kids, the answers were consistent. At the top of the list was our kids being bullied or suffering rejection; fear of kidnapping or abduction; negative peer pressure, especially in regard to alcohol, drugs, and sexual promiscuity; and concerns related to learning challenges, academics, or their future in general. Many Christian mothers added that they also worried about their children's spiritual lives and whether they would adopt the faith. Even so, our worry level pales in comparison to what the current generation of moms experiences.

A recent survey found that mothers today worry most about their children struggling with anxiety or depression as well as fearing that their children will be bullied, kidnapped, or abducted; have problems with drugs or alcohol; or get shot.[1] In fact, "nearly half [of polled mothers] (46 percent) report[ed] that they are 'extremely' or 'very' worried" about their child's mental health.[2] This worry didn't even get a mention among mothers in previous generations, but given the uptick in mental-health conditions among children and teens, these concerns are valid. The world that today's children face is complex and heavy. Smartphones, social media, and online communities give them access to far more of the world's pain and problems than any previous generation had. They are bombarded with more than they should have to bear. There's a reason for the saying *What you don't know can't hurt you.* The world I grew up in—and the one my children inhabited—was smaller and simpler than the world kids are navigating today.

Just as the proliferation of information can harm children's mental health, it also amplifies mothers' worries.

While it's true that "information is power," there is a threshold for its helpfulness. Information overload can paralyze us. Unfortunately, today's mothers are bombarded with information, whether they seek it or not. One minute you're looking for lodging for your upcoming beach vacation, and the next you're assaulted with links to articles on dry drowning, shark attacks, riptides, and collapsing sand pockets. Even if you only read the headlines, it's hard to forget the stories. Ignorance may be bliss, but what can we do with our worry if ignorance is no longer possible? How do we guard against living in a constant state of fear?

SEEING DANGER ACCURATELY

Most mothers know deep down that much of what they worry about will never come to pass. That reality alone, though, is not enough to ward off our worries. Our intense desire to protect our children from physical and emotional harm often results in a heightened sense of concern that eclipses logic and reason. Often our worry is disproportionate to the actual risk factor. Much of this is thanks to the lucrative business model of convincing mothers that the world is a dangerous place. Even though doom-and-gloom stories represent extremely rare events, terrifying headlines get more clicks and shares than their less fear-inducing counterparts. Marketers, businesses, and politicians reap rewards for employing emotionally manipulative tactics based on fearmongering. Fear sells.

One news story in particular ushered me into the motherhood-worry club with a storm of irrational fears. In October of 1987, Jessica McClure, an eighteen-month-old, was playing in her aunt's backyard when she fell into a narrow well shaft. The story of her rescue captured the nation's attention for the next fifty-eight hours as workers attempted to free her from the well shaft. The story had a happy ending: Jessica was rescued with relatively little harm done. She suffered a minor scrape on her head and an infection on her right foot that required reconstructive surgery.[3] But the story rattled me so much that, after my first child was born months later, I worried every time we visited my in-laws' East Texas ranch. What if my son fell into a hidden, unplugged well shaft during our visit? (Never mind that there were no well shafts on the property.)

That was 1987. With the prevalence of twenty-four-seven news, scrolling news tickers, and breaking-news notifications lighting up our phone screens today, we are subjected to a steady drip of bad news throughout the day. The rarer and more extreme the event, the more excessive the news coverage. The outsize noise devoted to rare events conditions us to begin believing that every negative occurrence poses a danger to us or our children.

As David Ropeik, a retired Harvard instructor and author of the book *How Risky Is It, Really?*, observes:

> Rare events with high emotional valence often get coverage disproportionate to their likelihood, further magnifying our fears. As a result of what the cognitive sciences call "the awareness heuristic"—a mental shortcut we use to quickly assess the likely frequency of things we don't know much about—the

more readily an event leaps to mind from our memory, or the more persistently it's in the news, the more emotionally powerful and probable it feels.[4]

Rather than buy into the fearmongering and *what-ifs* generated by a steady stream of isolated events, what if we focused on the bigger picture?

The truth is that there has never been a safer time to raise children in this country. Consider that out of one thousand babies born in 1800, a whopping 46 percent did not survive to their fifth birthdays. If you're doing the math, that is approximately 463 out of one thousand! Compare that to today, when there are just seven deaths per one thousand births in the United States. Child loss has declined steadily over the last two centuries, with the rare exceptions of the cholera pandemic and smallpox and yellow fever outbreaks in the 1870s and the Spanish flu pandemic in 1918.[5] Across child-age categories (ages one to four, five to fourteen, and fifteen to nineteen), mortality rates have fallen by nearly half since 1990.[6] Even with more cars on the road, 67 percent fewer teens died in auto-related fatalities in 2022 than in 1975.[7]

And that fear of kidnappings and abductions that's still high up on the list of worries among mothers today? According to the FBI, missing-person reports have been near record lows in recent years, falling 40 percent over the past twenty years. Among those who have gone missing, only 0.1 percent of cases have been due to kidnapping by strangers.[8]

When it comes to our children's safety, the possibility of a school shooting is at the top of the worry list for many mothers today. I had just entered Costco to do some shopping when news of Sandy Hook broke. I knew something was up when I saw people crowded around the dozens of TV sets at the front of the store, watching as the live news unfolded. Many moms, myself included, had tears streaming down our faces, awash with grief and devastation for the parents of the victims. We were terrified for our own children and grandchildren and the world in which they now live. While school shootings are a horrible recurrence in our country today, "the statistical likelihood of any given public school student being killed by a gun, in school, on any given day since 1999 [is] roughly 1 in 614,000,000."[9] (Of course, this does *not* negate the need for commonsense gun laws to help reduce these senseless tragedies, and we should continue to fight for stricter gun policies as well as an increase in mental-health programs to help deter future tragedies.)

When it comes to physical dangers, statistically speaking, our children have never been safer. In fact, children today are safer than children in any preceding generation. It is our nature to want to protect our children from harm, but we can go overboard if our default response is to Bubble Wrap our children to insulate them from the world.

Of course, worry isn't logical. Statistics alone can't help us maintain perspective and peace. Worry tends to reside in the recesses of our minds and, once triggered, seems to spiral as if it's on autopilot. To change this pattern, we have to do what we can to avoid worry triggers while also arming ourselves with a plan and then implementing it with intentionality.

ASKING YOUR WORRY A QUESTION

Years ago, I decided to install an outdoor security camera on the front of my house. Initially I loved the notification feature that alerted me to any movement in the general radius of my front door—but that feeling quickly waned as my phone erupted with false alerts throughout the day. I wanted to receive notifications of potential breaches in security, not nonstop, battery-draining clips of tree branches swaying in the wind, birds nesting in the eaves, and spiders spinning webs on my porch railing. I considered turning the notifications off altogether, but that would defeat the purpose of the camera. Fortunately, I found a solution in the app settings: a sensitivity feature. As you might guess, motion sensitivity was set on the highest option. I adjusted it, and—voilà—problem solved. A few false alerts still slip through from time to time, but overall, most of the notifications are related to actual people approaching the front door.

When it comes to motherhood worry, many of us have defaulted to the highest possible sensitivity setting, which means we live in a state of heightened response to false alerts. When our worry is easily triggered by false alerts, we find it increasingly hard to regulate our responses in a manner proportionate to an actual event or potential threat. Our bodies weren't meant to maintain a constant spike in cortisol. Over time, worry can affect our emotional well-being and manifest as anxiety, overprotection, distrust, pessimism, and a chronic sense of doom and gloom. It is a vicious cycle that needs to be broken.

If only we could adjust a sensitivity setting in our minds as quickly as we can on our phones! Regulating our radar for fear is far more difficult: We have to confront the source of our worry, over and over, and evaluate actual threat levels. This means taking our worry setting off autopilot and addressing each concern manually until we develop new ways of thinking and reacting to potential threats. A helpful question we can learn to ask ourselves is this: *What is the ultimate fear at the root of my worry?*

For the sake of this exercise, let's circle back to one of my original motherhood worries: the toddler who fell into the uncapped well shaft and my preoccupation with the same thing happening to my son at my in-laws' ranch. Even though it's been over three and a half decades, I can quickly identify the baseline fear at the root of my worry. Of course I was concerned about my son's safety and well-being, but underneath this rational motive was the fear that my son would suffer harm while on my watch, which would mean that I'd failed in my job as a mother. Can you relate? The false belief that *I'm a terrible mom if . . .* may not be at the forefront of our minds, but if we dig underneath recurring fears, we're probably going to find it lurking.

If we are going to dial down our sensitivity to false alarms, we must first address the misconception that we can protect our children from any and every threat of harm, both known and unknown, that may come their way. Also embedded in this lie is the belief that love equals constant protection. Protecting our children from threats (real or imagined) is not a binary. We are not neglectful or unloving parents just because our kids occasionally get injured. The truth is that we cannot have our eyes on our children every moment. We cannot predict the challenges, harms, and dangers our children may face over the course of their lives. Nor does God expect us to. We do the best we can with the capacity we've been given to watch over our children.

The truth of it is this: Sometimes they will fall down. They will get hurt. They will face danger. They will get sick. They will take risks. They will fail. They will sin. They will rebel. They will feel rejected. They will feel sad. No matter how much we love our kids, the options aren't either *never* or *always*. For good, loving parents, every single one of these things will happen *sometimes*—whether we worry or not.

Even when the worst happens, it is not because we've failed our children. If our aim is a perfect track record, we set ourselves up for failure. And I would go so far as to say that we also set our children up for failure. If we take on the role of bodyguard, fixer, controller, or preventer-in-chief, we will miss the joys of motherhood and raise children who grow up helpless and afraid. It's time to let ourselves off the hook of perfection as the marker of a good mom.

Once we calmly assess the actual threat level of the thing we're worrying about (rather than what we imagine the threat level to be), considering reasonable action steps can help us tamp down our internal response. A levelheaded and direct approach to the things we *can* do often loosens the grip of worry and anxiety. For example, when my daughter was going into high school, we decided to move her from a small private Christian school to a large public high school. She did not know anyone in her grade, and I was a neurotic mess. If I had asked my worry a question—*What is the ultimate fear at the root of my worry?*—I would have said that I was afraid I'd made a huge mistake in moving her out of the only school she'd ever known. If my daughter was unhappy, it was my fault. Or so I told myself.

Was my worry a false alarm? In part, yes, given that it was all-consuming. But there was also some truth to it. Of course a mother would worry about such a transition. It's hard to see your children walk into new or unfamiliar experiences. I couldn't control the ultimate course of events, but I could implement a few action steps to make the transition easier for both of us. I processed my fears openly with a mentor-friend, which helped me discern between reasonable concerns versus out-of-control anxiety. I connected with some mothers of freshmen at the school and initiated a few get-togethers before the school year started. My daughter ended up hitting it off with one of the girls, which helped alleviate her stress going into a new environment. I also committed to praying about the situation. Every time the fear felt heavy, I visualized myself handing the worry over to God.

The transition to public school was hard for my daughter, and it took some time for her to adjust. That is real life, and it wasn't the last time she had to adapt to a new environment. Life is full of challenges. Our children grow into healthy adults by facing them—not by being shielded from anything difficult, uncomfortable, or unpleasant. In the end, this transition strengthened my daughter's faith and reinforced the fact that with God's help she could do hard things. It taught me, too—that often the things we worry about being too hard or too big for our children to handle are the things that build their character and resilience.

What if your child suffers rejection, experiences heartbreak, or feels sad? Is God present in their times of sorrow? Can he draw them closer and comfort them? Of course he can!

If your child doesn't get into the college they want or struggles to figure out what to do with their life, is God able to work through whatever happens? Of course he is! His plans for your child may not match up with yours, but he can be trusted to bring good from the situation.

God will not leave or forsake us. Nor will he leave or forsake our children. Even if our worries come to pass, he is at work in every situation. What a comforting reminder to know that we are not alone.

CAST ALL YOUR CARES

One surefire way to notice that our worry has run amok is if we find ourselves in a downward spiral of *what-ifs*. You know the mess I was when my daughter was switching schools? I was stuck in that spiral. You've probably been there yourself.

- *What if* my child doesn't get the teacher I requested?
- *What if* my child doesn't make the team?
- *What if* my child caves in to peer pressure?
- *What if* my child feels sad and I'm not there to comfort him or her?
- *What if* my child struggles with mental health?

- *What if* my child gets bullied?
- *What if* my child doesn't get into a good college?
- *What if* my child gets hurt?
- *What if* my job, my schedule, or a life crisis prohibits me from spending as much time with my child as I want to?

It is perfectly normal to feel concern over the uncertainties related to *what-if*s. But concern most quickly escalates into worry when we dwell more on the fear of the unknown than our faith in the Known.

In Philippians 4:6-7, Paul says,

> Do not be anxious about anything, but in every situation, by prayer and petition, with thanksgiving, present your requests to God. And the peace of God, which transcends all understanding, will guard your hearts and your minds in Christ Jesus.

God invites us to bring our worries to him. In exchange, he offers "peace . . . which transcends all understanding." Peace instead of fear. Calm instead of chaos. Trust instead of control. How do we make the trade? We begin with *prayer and petition* and *thanksgiving*. What does that look like? To put it simply: We give the matter over to God. When worry becomes our default in a situation, we should pause to consider whether we're struggling to trust God. When we insist on basking in our worry, we are essentially saying to God, "Thanks for your offer, but I've got this."

But Jesus reminds us of a better way:

> "Therefore I tell you, do not worry about your life, what you will eat or drink; or about your body, what you will wear. Is not life more than food, and the body more than clothes? Look at the birds of the air; they do not sow or reap or store away in barns, and yet your heavenly Father feeds them. Are you not much more valuable than they? Can any one of you by worrying add a single hour to your life?
>
> ". . . But seek first his kingdom and his righteousness, and all these things will be given to you as well. Therefore do not worry about tomorrow, for tomorrow will worry about itself. Each day has enough trouble of its own."
>
> MATTHEW 6:25-27, 33-34

God sees things from a big-picture perspective. God cares about every part of his creation, even the birds—and he cares about us even more. That means, as much as we care for our children, God cares for them beyond what we could imagine possible. But he doesn't just care for our children. In 1 Peter 5:7, we are told to "cast all [our] anxiety on him because he cares for [*us*]" (emphasis added). We are just as important to God as our children are.

God loves you deeply. He never intended worry to be a standard part of the motherhood package. He offers peace in place of fear, but we have to be willing to take him up on the offer. He is worthy of our trust.

REFLECTION QUESTIONS

1. What tops your motherhood-worry list of *what-ifs*?

2. Think of a recent (or current) situation related to one or more of your children that left you preoccupied with worry. What question would you ask your worry to delve deeper into the root issue? What would the answer be?

3. How much less might you worry if you became more intentional about more accurately seeing dangers facing your children?

4. Reread Philippians 4:6-7:

   > Do not be anxious about anything, but in every situation, by prayer and petition, with thanksgiving, present your requests to God. And the peace of God, which transcends all understanding, will guard your hearts and your minds in Christ Jesus.

   Are you in the habit of bringing your worries to God? What hope do you find in this passage?

SIX

LESS STUFF, MORE MAGIC

The Grace of Simplicity

"Where your treasure is, there your heart will be also."
MATTHEW 6:21, CSB

"Are you and your family going anywhere fun over the summer?"

It was my daughter's last week of first grade, and we had invited one of her friends over for a playdate. As we drove home, I asked her friend about their summer plans—and my heart sank a little as the girl began to excitedly share about their upcoming trip to Disney World.

While I was certainly happy for her, Disney didn't fit into our budget. In fact, just the week before, my husband and I had gathered the kids to announce that we were going to vacation in Arkansas that summer, staying in cabins at two of the state parks. This was 1996, in the pre-internet era, so we laid out pamphlets depicting possible activities and allowed each of our kids to pick one. We ended up with horseback riding, visiting an alligator farm, and digging for diamonds at Crater of Diamonds State Park. And of course there would also be swimming and hiking. The kids seemed excited, and I was as well—until this moment in the car.

My daughter's friend began to list all the fun things she and her family were going to do at Disney World. The fun rides and the different parks. Breakfast with the Disney characters. My daughter, an aspiring princess, lit up as her friend described a princess makeover and party she and her sisters were going to attend. I focused on the road ahead, realizing I'd need to help my daughter unpack her disappointment later that evening.

And then my daughter spoke up from the back seat, and I could hardly believe my ears. With the excitement and exuberance of someone who had just been told they'd won a million dollars, my daughter said, "Well, guess where *we're* going?" She paused to build more anticipation. "We're going to . . . ARKANSAS!" She then proceeded to list the activities on our itinerary, clearly thinking she'd won the vacation jackpot. I could hardly contain my laughter when her friend responded, "Wow!! You're so lucky! When I get home, I'm going to ask my parents if we can go to Arkansas instead of Disney World."

As a mother, I put tremendous pressure on myself to provide a magical childhood, and nothing says "magical" more than a trip to Disney, right? Or so I thought until my daughter set me straight!

We all want to offer our children the world, and we all feel the pressure to deliver on that promise. Whether it's trips, extracurricular activities, toys, gadgets, or the like, we want to offer the best of the best in the hope that they will look back someday and remember a childhood filled with joy and happiness.

But this idea that we are responsible for delivering a magical childhood experience—with all the trips and gifts and toys that go along with it—is another motherhood lie. Exceptional is not the end goal.

ALL THE THINGS

I've heard it said that we manage our possessions or they will manage us. If you've ever wondered where you might fall on that scale, try packing up a house you've lived in for nearly three decades and moving to one with less storage space. This was my reality several years ago when my husband and I decided to sell the home we'd lived in for twenty-seven years and relocate to a small town in the Hill Country of Texas. In the process of packing up my home one room at a time, I was forced to accept that I had a problem: I had too much stuff. Much like a staged intervention by a group of caring friends, the move was my wake-up call. *Out of sight, out of mind* was no longer possible once everything was brought out into the open. I was busted, and it was humbling, to say the least.

Who has time to purge when you're in the thick of raising kids? Even if you did, more stuff would just replace what you purged anyway. I suppose there is logic in annual spring cleaning, but I never seemed to find the time or motivation to make it happen. It was all I could do to gather up the clothes my children had outgrown and drop them off at the local thrift store each year. I reasoned that I'd tackle the problem once they graduated and moved out, but here I was ten years later, and that day had never come. Not to mention that I had inherited more stuff when each of my children had graduated from college and lacked adequate space to store their belongings.

Culling my children's bedrooms proved harder than I imagined as I sorted through their closets and dressers, unearthing long-forgotten treasures that offered snapshots of their fleeting childhood years. One item at a time, I determined which items would graduate to the keepsake bin, which would be given away, and which would be relegated to the trash (I see you, participation trophies, honorable-mention ribbons, and board games with missing pieces!). And then there's the stuff in the TBD category. What do you do with half a dozen leather jackets from sports and cheer competitions? Or the multitudes of trophies that were once proudly displayed on bookshelves, their sheen now coated in a layer of dust after sitting atop a closet shelf for years? Ditto for the dance and cheer uniforms, the sports jerseys, and the colonial dress you personally sewed for Colonial Day? Or what about the multitudes of school projects that represented weeks of hard work and plenty of blood, sweat, and tears? Someone should create a black market for upcycled school projects that can be made available to the legion of desperate moms. Not to brag, but my son's third-grade rock-and-mineral project was impressive. We even scored an A on it. (Wait, did I say "we"? I meant "he"!)

As the keepsake pile grew bigger, I realized I wasn't contributing much to the discard pile. I knew my children wouldn't want many of the items, but each one triggered a sudden wave of nostalgia, taking me back to a season in their childhood—their interests, their activities, their bedtime cuddlies, their favorite books and treasures.

And then it hit me—it wasn't the items that held the value. It was the event or the memory each one represented. The items were nothing more than props that helped tell a bigger story: a mother's desire to offer her children the best childhood possible. If ever I doubted that I'd done enough, given enough, provided enough, and sacrificed enough to make their childhoods as memorable as possible, this was the proof. Or so I thought.

Mixed in with the nostalgia of the memories was a wave of conviction over the sheer excess of stuff. It was particularly distressing to see the big-ticket items that had each cost a small fortune but had a short shelf life. The game consoles and cartridges that often became outdated within a year and got replaced by more expensive game consoles that required different-sized cartridges. Stacks and stacks of board games, many of which had been played less than a handful of times. American Girl dolls and accessories that had held my daughter's interest for maybe a year before she retired them to a plastic bin in the corner of her room. A dress-up trunk with enough gear to outfit a dozen or more pint-size princesses. Pricey books from over a decade's worth of school book fairs, some of which hadn't ever been cracked open. And don't even get me started on the Beanie Babies collections (times three children, since sharing one collection would not have been a possibility). Among them were the retired ones that I had personally hunted down by cold-calling hospital gift shops and Cracker Barrel stores during the day while my children were in school. If that doesn't scream magical childhood, I don't know what does!

Even though I knew deep down that stuff doesn't equal love, I still fell prey to the lie that all the stuff and activities would contribute to my children remembering their childhoods as exceptional. The truth is that the clutter had taken a toll on my soul for years. The overstuffed closets with barely a square inch of floor space; dresser drawers packed so full they resisted when you tried to open them; a garage so packed to the brim with our children's sports paraphernalia and riding toys that there was no room for our cars.

I recently read that children in the United States make up approximately 3 percent of the population of children worldwide yet possess more than 40 percent of the toys purchased globally.[1] The average child in the United States receives seventy new toys a year.[2] Pressures to buy come from a multitude of sources, including savvy ad campaigns targeted directly to our children; online algorithms created to appeal to our desire to be exceptional mothers; peer pressure from other parents who have given up the fight; and—the hardest of all to resist—the begging and pleading of sad-eyed children who claim that they are the only ones who don't have said item, game, gadget, toy, trinket, or you-fill-in-the-blank. Our consumer-driven culture is all too happy to reinforce these messages by offering products and services to assist us in the task. From the moment our children are born, we are bombarded with endless advice, marketing campaigns for must-have gadgets, and a heavy dose of good, ol'-fashioned peer pressure to help us give our children an edge.

I recently discovered a product on Amazon that claims to give your child a head start before they even breathe their first breath. For a whopping $189, you can purchase a "prenatal education system" and strap an audio monitor onto your pregnant belly once a day to give your unborn baby a one-hour lesson. The company claims that their so-called prenatal education system will have a "lifelong impact," including a baby that is born "relaxed and alert," "nurse[s] readily," and "display[s] an increased ability to self-soothe."[3] Suffice it to say, there were plenty of customer reviews warning prospective buyers to "save your money." I laughed out loud at one parent review that read: "She came out of the womb screaming and kicking. . . . I have not seen any of the calmness and contentedness I was hoping for. Our baby appears to be a normal, crying and screaming baby."[4] It sounds like that mom would have been better served had she used the $189 on earplugs and a spa day!

Twenty years from now, our children will not remember the toys that filled their toy boxes or lined the shelves (or, let's be honest, the floor!) in their rooms. What they will remember most are the shared experiences, the family gatherings, their outdoor play and adventure, the people they loved, and those who loved them in return. In fact, Thomas Gilovich, a Cornell University psychology professor, has conducted multiple studies proving that "experiences, not belongings, are what elicit true feelings of happiness." Gilovich "argues that our memories of those experiences stick with us, whereas we ultimately adapt and get used to all the things we possess."[5] Perhaps most ironic is that supplying our children with too many toys is actually counterproductive.

A government-funded study on the impact on children of having too many toys found that "children become overwhelmed and over-stimulated and cannot concentrate on one toy long enough to learn."[6]

Truth be told, this isn't new news to most of us. I look back on my own parenting journey and remember the guilt I felt over the excess of toys in our home. Sometimes I gathered some up and donated them, but then birthdays and Christmas rolled around and we filled the empty space with more toys. It feels like a losing battle.

Most of us have witnessed this truth firsthand on Christmas morning or when our children celebrate their birthdays by shifting their attention from one new toy to another, oftentimes never spending enough time to unpack the full potential of each one and the pleasure it was meant to provide. Imagine the freedom we can experience if we embrace the truth that less might actually be best for our children—and truly more magical. Not to mention that it may be best for our mental health as well.

THE MENTAL TOLL OF TOO MUCH STUFF

Why do we keep buying into the propaganda that more stuff will deliver more happiness? Maybe because it does, briefly. Who hasn't experienced a buzz of euphoria (also known as dopamine) upon seeing Amazon packages sitting on the front porch? One-click buying, free shipping, fast delivery, better prices, and the ability to make free returns was a game changer for most of us. What's not to like? While unpacking our latest treasures, few of us have taken the time to unpack the real price we're paying for all these goods. It's affecting our souls. At some point, the dopamine buzz wears off, whether it's due to anxiety related to the credit-card statement that follows, guilt when items go unused or sit idly for long periods of time, frustration over the additional time required to manage or maintain yet more possessions, or the maddening process of returns that can quickly send you to a dark place if they don't go as planned. Or how about when you spend big bucks on a gift for your child and they end up liking the packaging more? We've all experienced a spending hangover at some point.

While our culture feeds us the lie that more money and possessions will lead to more happiness and satisfaction, studies indicate that overconsumption and clutter can have a negative impact on our mental health and overall well-being. A UCLA study analyzing thirty-two families found that when "the [surveyed] mothers discussed their messiest rooms—the ones filled with all the things meant to make life for them and their families better, easier and happier—the opposite seemed to occur. Their levels of cortisol, a stress hormone, spiked."[7] Another study found that women who considered their homes cluttered had high levels of cortisol while those who viewed their homes as well organized had lower levels.[8]

A *Time* magazine article highlights this reality:

> Today, about 1 in 6 Americans suffers from an anxiety disorder for a variety of reasons, something that appears to be not only a cause of our stuffocation but also an effect. To alleviate feelings

of anxiety, many of us shop, an act that has been shown to release dopamine in the brain, giving us a temporary feeling of euphoria. It's a sensation that we want to keep reliving, a sensation that can lead to overconsumption. But those anxious feelings can all come creeping back again once we get home and have to deal with all the stuff we've already bought.[9]

"'These objects that we bring in the house are not inert,' says UCLA anthropologist Elinor Ochs, who led a decade-long study on hyperacquisition. 'They have consequences.'"[10]

Clearly, a home filled with excess stuff can add to the stress load mothers already carry in the pursuit to be enough. And all that stress can, in turn, affect how you parent and the relationships you have with your children. Not to mention the impact our excess clutter has on the environment or the possibility that our stuff (especially fast fashion) is outsourced to workforces in developing nations that pay unfair wages.

If we want to break this vicious cycle, we must get to the heart of the problem rather than find a way for the problem to look prettier and more organized. Much like anything else we experience conviction over, a desire for something better is incomplete unless it's followed with repentance and change.

My move ended up being a catalyst to refocus my priorities and redefine my *enough*. However, my *enough* may not be your *enough*. It's possible overconsumption or excess is not an issue for you. I have one friend who is a true minimalist. You can actually walk into the walk-in closets in her home! She has unoccupied shelf space and empty hanging space in her master closet! If this is your gift, much of what I've written in this chapter may not be of benefit to you, but your perspective can benefit other mothers who wish to declutter their lives and don't know where to begin. A friend helped me organize my kitchen pantry after I moved, and it was a wonderful gift.

For others, maybe you just need a system of organization that will help alleviate the chaos in your home and reduce the stress. My father used to say, "A place for everything and everything in its place." Clearly, I didn't inherit that gene, but I can recognize the peace it would bring to live a more simplified life with less stuff to manage. I am not an expert when it comes to organizational tips, and it's safe to say that professional organizer Marie Kondo isn't going to call me for advice, but I've picked up some insights along the way. If you're like me and the thought of decluttering your entire home is overwhelming, here are a few tips and ideas you might consider:

- *Take it slow.* Start in one room and tackle one drawer, one cabinet, one bookshelf, one closet at a time. Rome wasn't built in a day, and you will set yourself up for failure if you attempt to do a massive purge of your home all at once.

- *Pull all the contents out into the open and divide them into one of four categories: Keep, Donate, Throw Away, and Decide.* If you haven't used an item in a year, consider donating it unless it has sentimental value. When the Donate bin is full, take it to your favorite thrift store or schedule a pickup. Involve your children to teach them the value of charitable giving.

- *Take "before" and "after" pictures of each area you organize, and put these pictures in an album on your phone to serve as a reminder of your progress.* This will also encourage momentum. When you're tempted to buy something you don't really need, look at the pictures in the album, or better yet, revisit the cleaned-up space. Talk about a dopamine buzz!

- *After you purge your children's toys, consider having a Swap Box—anytime they receive a new toy, they put a toy they no longer play with in the bin to donate.* Once you have purged your closets, consider doing the same thing when any item of clothing is purchased. If I get a new pair of shoes (my love language), I try to put a pair in a Donate bin I keep in my laundry room. I've also heard of a thirty-wear rule for buying new clothing items or shoes. If you don't think you'll wear it at least thirty times (with the exception of special-occasion wear), don't buy it.

- *Consider becoming a thrifter.* I love shopping at thrift stores and have found some amazing bargains on quality goods. If you are really daring, try shopping thrift stores for all clothing and home decor for several months. It's great for the environment and your pocketbook!

- *Consider spending less on your children's toys and instead gifting them with experiences you can share.* If you're up for a real challenge, try implementing a one-year toy break and plan a family trip with the money you save. Chances are good that your kids will receive plenty of toys from grandparents (guilty as charged!) and others on birthdays and holidays. Let your children be part of the trip-planning process, and keep a countdown calendar until the trip.

The purpose of this chapter isn't to persuade you to become a minimalist who forgoes all wants and only lives on absolute essentials. Everyone is different, and only you can determine what *enough* looks like in your family. The end goal is to put your possessions in their place—not just physically but also spiritually. Having homes that reflect the grace of simplicity yields more time, energy, and money to invest in the things that matter most.

WHERE IS YOUR TREASURE?

The ultimate remedy for our bent toward excess lies not in changing our habits but rather in changing our hearts. Jesus knew we would seek to fill our souls with things that don't have eternal value. In Matthew 6, he counsels,

> "Don't store up for yourselves treasures on earth, where moth and rust destroy and where thieves break in and steal. But store up for yourselves treasures in heaven, where neither moth nor rust destroys, and where thieves don't break in and steal. For where your treasure is, there your heart will be also."
>
> MATTHEW 6:19-21, CSB

Our relationship with our things is complicated. Whether we struggle with a tendency to buy too much for our children or for ourselves, it is necessary to take a deeper look into our hearts, particularly our definition of treasure.

Jesus also provides a sobering perspective on what we treasure in the parable of the rich fool:

> "A rich man's land was very productive. He thought to himself, 'What should I do, since I don't have anywhere to store my crops? I will do this,' he said. 'I'll tear down my barns and build bigger ones and store all my grain and my goods there. Then I'll say to myself, "You have many goods stored up for many years. Take it easy; eat, drink, and enjoy yourself."'"
>
> LUKE 12:16-19, CSB

At first appearance, it would be easy to conclude that the rich man was simply trying to find a practical solution for his harvest. He had an excess of grain and not enough storage space to accommodate the surplus. His solution? Tear down his barns and build bigger ones. Makes sense to me. If money were no object, I'd dial a contractor to come tear down my undersized pantry and build one of those cavernous butler's pantries with a sink, extra refrigerator, open shelving to display my wedding china (which I've used three times), and extra countertop space for food prep in the rare event I should cook.

But Jesus saw this situation differently. He didn't offer the man a thumbs-up or a pat on the back for his resourcefulness.

In fact, Jesus' response should remind us that God's thoughts are not ours and our ways are not his (Isaiah 55:8).

> "But God said to him, 'You fool! This very night your life is demanded of you. And the things you have prepared—whose will they be?'
> "That's how it is with the one who stores up treasure for himself and is not rich toward God."
> LUKE 12:20-21, CSB

Jesus offers us a glimpse into God's heart when it comes to putting too high a priority on hoarding possessions. He wasn't condemning possessions (or even butler's pantries!)—he was making a statement about the priority our possessions hold in our lives. The rich fool revealed his true allegiance by focusing his attention on "stor[ing] up treasure for himself" rather than being "rich toward God." His surplus of grain was at the forefront of his mind, consuming far too much of his time and attention. He had become possessed by his possessions. While the world might view the fool as rich in earthly treasures, God saw him as bankrupt in the treasures that matter most.

For many of us, stuff has become part of our motherhood identity. In our zeal to offer our children the very best, though, we often overlook what's truly best for them. And we end up taking on more stress in the process.

You get to decide what defines *treasure* in your home and, better yet, how you pass that treasure along to your children. The best childhood you can offer your children is one that prioritizes heavenly treasures over earthly ones. It is a home filled with love and laughter, open communication, humility, the ability to own your sins and ask forgiveness, and above all, a commitment to live out the greatest commandments according to Jesus: love God and love others (Mark 12:28-34). A home built on the right foundation brings peace and stability to the lives of all who inhabit it. *That* is the brand of magic I hoped to leave to my children. Even though I didn't always get it in the right balance, I pray that that was ultimately the takeaway.

DOWN THE ROAD

I've heard it said that you never see a U-Haul behind a hearse. In 1 Timothy 6:7, Paul reminds us, "We brought nothing into the world, and we can take nothing out" (CSB). Nothing drives this truth home more than the task of parsing through the estate of a loved one who has passed away. When I lost my mother, I agreed to help her husband with this difficult task. My mother did a good job of purging over the years, yet it was still sobering to see all her possessions. I kept the items that had sentimental value, many of which had belonged to my grandparents and had been passed to my mother upon their deaths. One by one, I placed various treasures into a plastic bin: photo albums containing her childhood pictures and our family pictures; her silver flatware; a half-used crystal bottle of her favorite perfume; keepsakes given to her by me or my brother; and jewelry, some of which I would keep and some I would pass down to my daughter, granddaughters, and niece. On my way home, I dropped off my mother's clothes and shoes at a thrift shop.

When I brought the bin of treasures inside, I added a shoebox of my father's possessions to the bin and paused before putting the lid on top. My brother (and only sibling) had passed away several years prior, and my father shortly after him, so I felt a strange responsibility as the remaining caretaker of what was left from my family of origin. And that's when it hit me. My mother's life, my father's life, and what possessions remained from the family of my youth were in a lone plastic bin that would reside on a top shelf in a storage closet. That's what all this comes to. The buying, the gathering, the collecting of earthly treasures that will ultimately be left behind for someone else to deal with. A portion will be divided among heirs, but most will be sold, donated, or tossed. It's a humbling thought but also a freeing one. Considering the fate of our possessions releases their present power over us.

Someday my children will parse through what's left of my earthly possessions. If they find some sentimental treasure that sparks a memory or reminder of me and it makes it into a keepsake bin, that's great, but it's not how I ultimately hope to be remembered. I want my children to remember our shared experiences, my unconditional love for them, and most importantly, the valuable legacy of a faith in Jesus Christ. In other words, I want them to remember the long-term treasures in heaven that made their mother truly rich. I have a long way to go, but I keep the image of that plastic bin at the forefront of my mind as I attempt to invest less in stuff and more in Jesus.

REFLECTION QUESTIONS

1. In what ways have you bought into the motherhood lie that you owe your child a magical childhood filled with the "best" of everything?

2. Does excess stuff have an impact on your mental health? If yes, in what way?

3. How would you answer the question *Where is your treasure?* How does that affect the kind of childhood you hope to offer your children?

4. What changes, if any, do you feel led to make as a result of reading this chapter?

SEVEN

YOU MATTER TOO

The Grace of Being Kind to Yourself

Keep good company, read good books, love good things, and cultivate soul and body as faithfully as [you] can.
LOUISA MAY ALCOTT

In the process of packing up my home, I came across a program for a women's event I had been part of many years ago. The event offered workshops you could choose over the two-day period in addition to keynote sessions and worship time. Among the list of workshops were those on topics related to making memories with your children, learning your husband's love language, dealing with a strong-willed child, teaching your children to pray, cultivating a happy home, grocery shopping on a budget, assessing your child's personality type, being a supportive wife, and many more. Women had a wide variety of options to choose from—but now I noticed one glaring omission. There was not a single workshop addressing self-care. Most focused on funneling your time and attention into serving others, and in particular on meeting the needs of your husband and children.

It's important to note that part of the program for first-time attenders at this particular event—whether married, single, divorced, widowed, childless, struggling with infertility, or empty nesting—was to attend predetermined core workshops addressing marriage, raising children, submission to your husband, and the role of the Holy Spirit in the Christian life. While I learned many wonderful truths while serving on this event's ministry team, I felt a deep sadness over the general assumption that motherhood (and marriage) were a woman's highest calling and chief purpose in life. No wonder there were no workshops on self-care. If a woman's identity is based on her status as a wife and mother and her ultimate purpose is to serve her husband and children, her self is no longer relevant. She is merely an extension of them.

In fact, I don't recall even hearing the term *self-care* until many years later, especially within conservative Christian circles. Even then I questioned the notion and wondered if it was selfish for a mother to focus on herself, rationalizing that there would be years to do so in the aftermath of raising children. Based on the program in my hand, reflective of so much of the teaching I had absorbed within my circle of faith, it shouldn't come as a surprise that the idea of caring for myself was a struggle for me.

My personal experience with burnout as the result of years of serving my family and my ministry and tending to the needs of everyone but myself led me to reevaluate many teachings related to a woman's identity and purpose. My turning point came in understanding that God doesn't call women to sacrifice themselves on the altar of marriage or motherhood. Our needs are important too. We matter to God—so our well-being should matter to us.

CREATE MARGIN

One of the greatest lessons I learned in my recovery phase from burnout was the concept of margin from author Richard Swenson. Margin, he says, is "the space between our load and our limits."[1] Much of my burnout was related to the lack of space in my daily routines to accommodate unanticipated events or, for that matter, to care for myself. Think of margin as a buffer zone intended to provide wiggle room throughout the day to readjust our plans or reset our minds. Discovering margin was one of the greatest gifts I gave myself in my pursuit of prioritizing self-care. If there is no space available to practice self-care, it remains a lofty ambition rather than a reality. Self-care relies on margin.

Margin may seem impossible to practice when the bulk of our days are consumed with the care of our children. It is not as if we can add more hours to the day. Creating margin is about being more deliberate about the choices we make. Often, we fill our days with activities that we reason will benefit our children but which end up being detrimental to our own mental health.

If you discover that you have no time for margin on any day throughout your week, you are headed for burnout. If you have a few days with a small block of time for margin, and you don't feel frazzled and worn out with the current pace, carry on. But if you are consistently overwhelmed or exhausted, your load has exceeded your limit. The key will be determining your capacity and the amount of time you need to reset. Another important consideration is whether you have support to help divide and conquer the various family activities. If you don't have support, you need to build even more margin into your schedule.

If you determine you need more margin, look over your current list of activities. Which fall into the category of "negotiable"? Does your daughter really need to participate in a dance program that requires multiple practices throughout the week? Does your son truly have to be involved in more than one sport at a time? If you have multiple children in after-school activities, could you shift to a one-child-per-season plan to help lighten the load? Or maybe block off entire seasons to give the family a break. (I promise, your children will be fine if they skip a year of extracurricular activities!)

Other ways to implement a margin buffer include

- looking over each day in advance to determine which events or activities can be scrapped if you need to redeem some time;
- choosing *good enough* over *exceptional*, whether it's the dinner menu, the time you spend tidying your house, or which items on your to-do list get done;
- asking yourself, *Will this activity stretch me too thin and lead to exhaustion and bitterness?* before saying yes to something;
- paying attention to physical, emotional, and mental cues that signal that you are at capacity and in need of self-care; and

- intentionally scheduling self-care activities, just as you would schedule other activities you deem important for your children or the whole family.

The benefits of margin are endless, but it will take intentionality and discipline to make it a priority in your life. Creating margin is the first step of kindness to yourself in the season of motherhood. It helps make space for you to be a person who matters—apart from your role as a mother and wife. When you carve out margin in your schedule, you acknowledge that you exist not to be needed but to be loved by God.

PRIORITIZE SELF-CARE

I realize it is difficult to say no to your children so you can say yes to margin. But kindness to yourself—creating space in your schedule not just for a less hurried pace but also for your needs and desires—isn't selfish. Our Creator calls us to live out our identity in him—which we can't do if our whole lives are built on the identity of "caregiver for everyone else."

If you already have blocks of time scheduled throughout the week (alone time, hobbies, girls' night out, book clubs, Bible studies, etc.), I applaud you! Resist the temptation to scrap activities that give you life so you can squeeze in more activities for your children. If self-care is a struggle for you, I encourage you to reflect more deeply on why that is. Maybe your mother didn't model self-care and therefore passed along the motherhood lie that a mother's needs always come last. Or perhaps you absorbed the toxic teaching that self-care is selfish and, as a result, feel guilty addressing your own needs. Or maybe you've bought into the busyness lie that more activities lead to a fulfilling life, despite the fact that you're running on an empty tank. Tap into your resistance to practicing self-care, and refuse to believe the lie that your well-being doesn't matter.

I know *self-care* can seem like an oxymoron in the chaotic years of raising children. For many moms who are already exhausted from the pace, it becomes one more to-do item—and it feels like the priority that can easily be dropped to the bottom of the list. But taking care of yourself—not merely existing and surviving—is vital to your physical, mental, and spiritual health.

You know that flight-attendant instruction to place the oxygen mask over your own face before helping someone else? The principle holds true for motherhood, too. If your child's needs always come before your own, you will run out of steam and have little to nothing left to give. Some seasons of motherhood are busier than others, but you should always have margin—if only a few minutes each day—to squeeze in something that refreshes you, fills your emotional and relational tank, or simply gives you a moment to breathe in peace.

I'm reminded of an afternoon when I was watching my oldest granddaughter, who was about two and a half years old at the time. I asked her if she wanted to do something, and she put her hand up and said, "Mimi, I need some space." I burst out laughing—because I knew she had picked the phrase up from my daughter.

Moms need some space from time to time. Let your children know from the time they are young that sometimes you need a break. In doing so, you model that they are not the center of your life and that your needs are important too.

I know that creating space for self-care may be particularly hard for some moms. Some are single parents, without another adult around to rely on. Others may have spouses who work long hours or who are disengaged or unsupportive. If that's you, I am so sorry. I know you're already stretched beyond your capacity, and that makes self-care particularly hard to come by. But you need it just as much as any other mom, if not more. What if you prioritized a creative solution to allow yourself some alone time? Maybe you can trade childcare with a friend and have a night on your own once a month. Or perhaps you can find ways to make space for something you love even when you're with your children, like reading a book while they play at the park or watch a favorite show. Even if your children are young, you can typically find something to distract them with for a short period of time while you reset and catch your breath. Maybe it's during nap time, or if that stage is over, a quiet-time period where your children learn the healthy balance of stilling themselves and playing alone.

Self-care looks different for each of us. You know best what helps you reset in the chaos of motherhood. Here are a few ideas to help get you started.

Physical Self-Care

- Do your best to eat food that makes you feel good (i.e., food that is nourishing rather than depleting) and drink plenty of water throughout the day.

- Walk around your neighborhood with or without your children. Even better if you can do it with a friend!
- Buy a set of weights to use while watching a show or the news.
- Have a few strength-building or cardio exercises you can do as time allows to get your heart pumping (planks, lunges, push-ups, jumping jacks, calf stretches, etc.).
- If your kids are old enough, engage them in an activity and grab a quick catnap.
- Find a responsible teen in your neighborhood who can watch your kids when you need a break.
- Treat yourself to a mani-pedi or an at-home spa day.
- Schedule a night away at a hotel or somewhere special where you can relax.

Mental Self-Care

- Read or listen to an interesting book or podcast that leaves you feeling uplifted.
- Have coffee with a friend.
- Reduce your time on social media and other technology.
- Find a group of like-minded moms to meet with on occasion.
- Stay in touch with your closest friends and consider occasionally calling rather than texting.
- Create a designated sitting space in your home—like in your bedroom or outdoor patio—with a comfortable chair, soft throw, twinkle lights, and your favorite candle.

- Buy flowers for yourself just because.
- Go to a movie alone.
- Sign up for an online master class that interests you and enjoy it as time permits.
- Start a puzzle and work on it from time to time.
- Take up a new hobby (embroidery, woodworking, bird watching, learning a foreign language, researching your ancestry, etc.) and enjoy it as time allows.
- Play a game on your phone or tablet to stimulate your brain. If you're limiting time on electronics, try a puzzle book or game instead.

Spiritual Self-Care

- Commit to read through a book of the Bible or find a daily devotional to help keep you in the Word.
- Find an older, godly mentor who can meet with you regularly in person.
- Join a Bible study. If time doesn't allow for a formal group, find a Bible-reading plan that can be done at your own pace.
- Play uplifting worship music in the background throughout your day.
- Get involved in a local church and take advantage of childcare during services.
- Pray daily. Don't just pray for your children's needs. Ask God for strength. Tell him what's on your mind. Touch base with him throughout the day and send up "flare prayers" as needed.

- Praise daily. Try to cultivate the habit of thanking God for those you encounter throughout the day and for the blessings in your life.

This list is certainly not comprehensive; there are many ways to practice self-care. Self-care is personalized. What works for you may not work for someone else. The key is to find out what helps you reset physically, mentally, and spiritually. An intentional practice of self-care will help you define an identity outside motherhood and remind you that God created you to be more than a mom. Most mothers will spend more years in the aftermath of raising their children than in the thick of it. Do the work now to be able to step into a fulfilling life then. View self-care as a necessary investment in the future.

PURSUE COMMUNITY

My refugee mom friends truly live by the adage *It takes a village to raise a child*. Most of the first-generation families left their parents behind to offer better lives to their children in a country unfamiliar to them. They don't have the benefit of a mother or grandmother nearby to help when they need support. Many said goodbye to their family members when they came to the United States knowing it was unlikely they would see them in person again. In the absence of extended family to lighten the childcare load, the whole refugee community pitches in to get the job done.

When I visit, I'll often find several mothers spending time together in their small apartments. Their toddlers play with hand-me-down toys on the living-room floor while the mothers catch up over cups of coffee or hot tea, many with infants strapped to their chests sleeping peacefully. When it's nap time, they often put their kids down in the bedroom and continue their visit. There is no sense of urgency, no rushing out the door to carpool or run errands, no checking their phones while engaged in conversation. They are present in the moment and there for one another. Every time I witness this scene, I feel a twinge of sadness that face-to-face visits among mothers have nearly become extinct, replaced by short, choppy text messages sent on the fly or quick social-media posts to troubleshoot parenting issues. This is not true support. My refugee friends model what support looked like for mothers in generations past: Moms were surrounded by a community of family members, friends, and neighbors. But Americans have become an increasingly mobile population. Many of us live far from our families of origin, and we may not even know our neighbors. Our societal emphasis on individualism discourages us from thinking we need to replace that lost support system. It's no wonder so many moms today are lonely!

We are wired for community. But these days—despite technological advances that offer us around-the-clock, constant contact with people—moms have never felt more alone. If raising children takes a village, the village has moved online or left town altogether.

So I'm encouraging you: Reestablish the village. Make intentional choices to build community. I encourage you to seek out a small, core group of real-life friends (and a mentor or two) to be your first line of defense when you need support and encouragement. There is nothing wrong with tapping into social media for motherhood support from time to time, but it should not be your go-to for connection. I know the thought of finding a solid support group of friends can be overwhelming for some, given that most moms are already short on time and exhausted from investing so much of their energy into their relationships with their husbands and children. Your attempts may be hit or miss as you seek these friends, but the future reward will make the present investment more than worth it.

If you don't know where to begin to find a core group, consider joining a small group at your church, looking for a book club, or finding a Bunco group. Maybe you seek out intentional time with a mom or group of moms you've volunteered with at your child's school or enjoyed visiting with on field trips. Maybe you invite a couple of moms from a local online group you're part of to grab coffee or do a park playdate once a week. Be sure to find mothers who offer a safe place to be honest about the struggles of motherhood rather than those who lengthen the how-to-be-a-better-mother list.

I am a big believer in the local church. It may take some time to find a group that aligns with your values and priorities, but don't give up the search. If no such group exists, consider starting one or finding a mentor who will lead it. Once your group is established, try to be intentional about scheduling face-to-face time. Know that things will come up (sick kids, scheduling conflicts, etc.), but make the effort to meet as consistently as possible.

Also consider asking an older, godly woman you respect if you can meet on a regular basis. I have met with younger moms over the years, and I am always as equally blessed as they are by these mentor-mentee relationships. When my children were young, I was on the receiving end of a small mothers' group that met in the home of an older, godly woman. It was a life-changing experience, and even though it was several decades ago, I still think about truths my mentor taught me. Many empty-nest moms have margin and are looking for ways to fill the gaps in their lives. It could be a win-win situation for you both.

Motherhood can feel very lonely at times. Having a few ride-or-die friends who know you well and have your back will help reduce your loneliness. And finding a mentor or two and being involved in multigenerational women's groups can provide encouragement and community support—all while reminding you that there is life after motherhood and much to look forward to in the future.

BE KIND TO YOURSELF

If creating margin, prioritizing self-care, and pursuing community are the outward expressions of self-compassion, taking back control of your negative inner critic is the vital inner work to help you practice these steps and reinforce that you matter too.

You know that quiet, accusatory voice—the one that whispers, *You are not enough*? Most of us have grown so used to it that we hardly notice it anymore.

- *I should have lost this baby weight by now.*
- *Why can't I handle the load like others?*

- *Will my house ever be organized? It's no wonder I can't find anything.*
- *I'm a horrible mother for letting my kids have this much time on the tablet, but I really need a break.*
- *Other moms seem to find time to exercise, so why can't I?*
- *My kids are entitled, and it's all my fault.*
- *Why is my child struggling in school? I'm sure it's because I haven't spent enough time helping them with their homework.*

I'll confess, I've got a lot of experience when it comes to negative self-talk. It comes along with the pressures of motherhood—that feeling that we have to get everything right, that we have to fit a certain mold and keep a certain kind of home, that our children have to be consistently polite and obedient to reflect well on our parenting. Inevitably, that perfect picture falls apart in little pieces along the way. And that's when the nagging whispers begin.

Negative self-talk is not exclusive to mothers. Neuroscientists claim that for most of us our brains default to negativity bias, or a tendency to assume the worst possible outcome rather than focus on the positive.[2] When negative self-talk becomes chronic, we create a false narrative about ourselves. Eventually, we develop neural pathways that reinforce our negative thinking, and before long, it is a well-established habit. Much like the routines we perform on autopilot each day, we hardly realize we're doing it.

The good news is that our brains can be rewired over

time. As we acknowledge the negative thoughts and redirect the narrative, we retrain our brains to counterbalance our negativity bias. This takes intentionality and practice.

Cultivate the habit of being kind to yourself. Practice positive self-talk each day. This isn't being self-absorbed or arrogant—it's learning to see yourself through God's compassionate eyes, to measure your decisions not by perfection but by grace. As Proverbs 18:21 reminds us, "the tongue has the power of life and death," so speak words that bring life to your soul rather than death.

Catch yourself when you are engaging in negative self-talk, and redirect the conversation. Better yet, stop and imagine how God might speak to you, then say that back to yourself. For example, if you are frustrated about weight you have gained since having children, acknowledge out loud that God made your body strong and resilient and that he also designed a woman's body to change over time. One of my greatest regrets is the amount of time I invested in hating my body or appearance as a young mother. Even as I am growing older, I am still in the process of changing the narrative I tell myself.

I want to share a three-step tool that has helped me cultivate a new motherhood narrative about myself—a kinder and more compassionate one. I have labeled it *CPR* because it can breathe life into a new thought habit related to my identity—not just as a mother but, more importantly, as a child of God. Here are the three steps of CPR:

- **Capture:** When you find yourself engaging in negative self-talk, pause and capture the thought. In taking the time to acknowledge it, you bring the negative thought out of the shadows of your subconscious and short-circuit a lapse into shame and guilt.

> We demolish arguments and every pretension that sets itself up against the knowledge of God, and we take captive every thought to make it obedient to Christ.
> **2 CORINTHIANS 10:5**

- **Pivot:** Turn away from the expectations and opinions of others and pivot toward God. He does not hold you to the same impossible standards as the culture. He is for you, not against you.

  > If our hearts condemn us, we know that God is greater than our hearts, and he knows everything.
  > **1 JOHN 3:20**

- **Renew:** Take a minute to renew your mind and reword your negative self-talk into a positive statement that centers on grace rather than condemnation. If possible, say it out loud, paying attention to your tone. Our inner voice can tend to speak to us with judgment and disgust. If you struggle with this, ask yourself how you might respond to a dear friend who spoke that way to herself. Or better yet, consider how you might respond to your own child if they were to express that they were not enough. Your tone would likely be one of kindness and compassion.

End with a quick word of encouragement, such as "Attagirl!" "You've got this!" or "Stay the course!"

> Do not conform to the pattern of this world, but be transformed by the renewing of your mind. Then you will be able to test and approve what God's will is—his good, pleasing and perfect will.
> **ROMANS 12:2**

> Finally, brothers and sisters, whatever is true, whatever is noble, whatever is right, whatever is pure, whatever is lovely, whatever is admirable—if anything is excellent or praiseworthy—think about such things.
> **PHILIPPIANS 4:8**

Here's what CPR might look like on days when you are overwhelmed and at capacity:

- *I am doing the best job I possibly can given the energy and resources I have at this time. I am a good mother. God's grace is sufficient for me. I am proud of myself for _____.*

> He said to me, "My grace is sufficient for you, for my power is perfected in weakness."
> **2 CORINTHIANS 12:9, CSB**

Or on days when you blow it and feel like a horrible mother:

- *I am not perfect. It is human nature to make mistakes from time to time.*

> I am sure of this, that he who started a good work in [me] will carry it on to completion until the day of Christ Jesus.
>
> **PHILIPPIANS 1:6, CSB**

Old habits die hard, so it will take time to rewire your self-talk. A hallmark study on habit forming in 2009 found that it takes an average of sixty-six days for a new habit to stick. For some it will take less time and for others more time.[3] Stick with it and don't give up. Before long, your thoughts won't run down the same negative track—instead, your first impulse will be to capture negative thoughts, pivot away from the world's expectations and toward God, and renew your mind to center on God's grace.

Each of us is a work in progress. God is not sitting in the heavens grumbling over your performance as a mother. He sees the whole picture of you who are. And he offers you grace and mercy when you stumble—so learn to offer yourself the same.

Creating margin, prioritizing and practicing self-care, and being kind to yourself rest on the foundation of believing you matter to God first and foremost as his daughter, not just as a mother. When you see God as a loving Father and view yourself through his eyes of unconditional love and grace, you can't help but come to the natural conclusion that you matter too.

REFLECTION QUESTIONS

1. Do you feel you have enough margin in your life to practice self-care? If not, what steps might you take to build a margin buffer into your daily routine?

2. Is the concept of self-care difficult for you to justify? If so, what might be the reason?

3. How are you doing when it comes to physical, mental, and spiritual self-care? What are some ways you can practice self-care in these areas?

4. Do you have a core group of friends you feel safe with and who have your back? If not, what steps might you take to establish a core friend group?

5. Do you struggle with negative self-talk? Using the CPR tool (*c*apture, *p*ivot, *r*enew), share a recent example of negative self-talk and a kinder version of speaking to yourself.

EPILOGUE

MORE THAN ENOUGH

As we come to a close, I know we have covered a great deal of information. I applaud you for making it this far when you have so much on your plate as it is. I hope you have not felt overwhelmed but rather encouraged that you can lay down the burden of inflated "good mother" overexpectations. You can step back from the struggle to be a perfect mother. Whether you wrestle with a misplaced sense of identity, a heavy burden of false guilt, motherhood comparison and the judgment that often results, chronic busyness that robs you of the ability to be present, worry over the *what-if*s, pressure to deliver an exceptional childhood, or a lack of self-care in the wake of meeting the needs of everyone else, I pray you feel motivated and equipped to make necessary changes to set you on a course of healing, hope, and freedom. Know that I see you. And more importantly, know that God sees you.

If I could go back and chat with my younger mom self, I would offer empathy, grace, and tenderness to that young, vulnerable mother who was hanging on to her sanity by a thin, fraying thread. I would tell her it's okay to be less than perfect. It's okay to not have it all together. It's okay to have weaknesses and shortcomings. It's okay to make mistakes. In fact, *all that is perfectly normal.* I would remind her that God is aware of her exhaustion, self-doubt, and the constant burden she carries to measure up to an impossible standard—a standard he never endorsed. I would hug her tight and reassure her that God sees her through a more compassionate lens, one coated in grace and filtered through his mercy. I would implore her to see herself through that same lens.

It may be too late to have that conversation with my younger mom self, but it's not too late to have it with you. This book is that conversation, and I pray it will be an ongoing balm to your soul, regardless of where you are in your motherhood journey.

You picked up this book for a reason. So through these final pages, let me speak to you right where you are:

- You are more than a mom.
- Your identity rests in being a much-beloved child of God.
- God has given you value and purpose apart from being a mother.
- He has already declared you good enough.
- Go forth and live in that grace.
- It is all you need.
- And it is more than enough.

APPENDIX

WHAT THE BIBLE SAYS ABOUT IDENTITY IN CHRIST

*From "Your Identity in Christ: How God Sees You"
by Brittany Yesudasan*[1]

You don't have to take anyone's word for it. Actually, God wants you to find out for yourself by reading his Word. It is important that you go to the Bible to find out how he feels about you. Your identity should never be based on a hope or a guess. God gave us his Word, the Bible, so you can know him and know who he is making you to be in him.

> You are no longer foreigners and strangers, but fellow citizens with God's people and also members of his household.
> **EPHESIANS 2:19**

You are a member of God's household, not a stranger. If you follow Christ, you belong in God's household and with his people.

In this passage, Paul is encouraging followers of Christ to remember that they are all part of one family. They are to be unified with each other. You can only experience this if you understand that you are a legitimate child of God. You are part of his family.

> God is able to bless you abundantly, so that in all things at all times, having all that you need, you will abound in every good work.
> **2 CORINTHIANS 9:8**

As a child of God, you have been blessed and are being provided for. God is able to provide you with everything you need in Christ. He is the owner of everything and the giver of all good things.

> See what great love the Father has lavished on us, that we should be called children of God! And that is what we are! The reason the world does not know us is that it did not know him.
> **1 JOHN 3:1**

In Christ, you are loved. Your identity is that of a child of God. This Bible verse comes from a chapter that warns against the temptation to stray from God into sin. You can resist sin by remembering that God has the best for his children. He offers you more than the world ever could. You are complete in his love.

> "The LORD your God is with you,
>   the Mighty Warrior who saves.

> He will take great delight in you;
> in his love he will no longer rebuke you,
> but will rejoice over you with singing."
>
> **ZEPHANIAH 3:17**

Jesus delights in you. You are not just accepted or put up with. You are welcomed into his family with delight.

When correction comes, it lasts for a short time because the goal is for it to help you reflect God's holy character more accurately. He delights in you so much that he is making you more like him day by day.

> God made him who had no sin to be sin for us, so that in him we might become the righteousness of God.
>
> **2 CORINTHIANS 5:21**

You have God's righteousness. You experience his goodness and rightness because of what Christ did on the cross. This was given to you, and you are called righteous by the Lord of the universe.

You can live in light of the righteousness you have been given. It not only allows you to approach God with confidence but also allows you to be an ambassador to others around you. Because your righteousness is not earned but freely given through faith in Jesus, you can share this gift with others and invite them to be God's righteousness too.

> Bear with each other and forgive one another if any
> of you has a grievance against someone. Forgive as
> the Lord forgave you.
> **COLOSSIANS 3:13**

You are forgiven. If you are a follower of Christ, you have become God's child because the Lord has forgiven you for the sin you have committed against him.

As someone who is forgiven, you can now freely forgive others. God has extended grace—that is, undeserved favor—to you. You can extend that grace to others around you.

> We are God's handiwork, created in Christ Jesus to
> do good works, which God prepared in advance for
> us to do.
> **EPHESIANS 2:10**

You were created with a purpose. God had specific intentions for your life when he brought you into the world. First and foremost, your purpose is to know him and glorify him. Then you can engage in other good works that will bring God glory and grow your own faith.

You were saved from great sin. Now, as a child of God, you can walk with God and do great good through his work in you.

> If anyone is in Christ, the new creation has come:
> The old has gone, the new is here!
> **2 CORINTHIANS 5:17**

In Christ, you are a new creation. God has made you new. The old things that used to define you have been taken away. God used to identify you as an enemy, but now he knows you as a child. You who were a sinner are now righteous.

You are new because through Jesus your sin has been paid for. You have been restored to right standing before God.

> You are a chosen people, a royal priesthood, a holy nation, God's special possession, that you may declare the praises of him who called you out of darkness into his wonderful light.
> **1 PETER 2:9**

You are special to God. You have been chosen by him. This verse comes from a passage that talks about how Christ was rejected by many. But by faith in Jesus, through the power of the Holy Spirit, if you trust in Jesus, you are part of his holy, chosen people.

You can rid yourself of things that are part of the old you, part of the darkness, such as deceit, hypocrisy, envy, and slander because you have been brought into wonderful light.

ACKNOWLEDGMENTS

I am immensely grateful for the team who helped make this book a reality. To my agent, Don Gates—thank you for your steady guidance all the way from concept to contract. To the crew at NavPress—even though we are new to one another, I have no doubt you are the perfect publisher to shepherd this message. I'm honored to be among your stable of authors. To my editor, Caitlyn Carlson—you saw the potential of this book the first time you read the proposal and boldly challenged me to expand the message to your generation of mothers, and here we are! Thank you for your wisdom, insight, and encouragement along the way.

As in any book I've written in the past, I want to acknowledge my husband, Keith. Thank you for being a true partner who faithfully supported me as I reexamined and untangled previously held beliefs related to a woman's primary identity. Most of all, thank you for your willingness to unpack them with me—our marriage is all the stronger for it.

And finally, I am grateful for every one of you who picked up this book and trusted me on this journey. I pray you have found freedom in God's abundant grace of *good enough*.

NOTES

INTRODUCTION | TOO MUCH AND NEVER ENOUGH

1. Christin Perry, "8 Signs You're Suffering from Depleted Mother Syndrome and How to Cope," *Parents*, updated January 9, 2025, https://www.parents.com/depleted-mother-syndrome-8717198.
2. Barna Group, *Motherhood Today: The State of Moms and What It Means for the Church* (Ventura, CA: Barna and The MomCo, 2023), 8, https://www.barna.com/motherhood-today-free-digital-report.
3. Barna Group, *Motherhood Today*, 10.
4. *House Calls with Dr. Vivek Murthy*, podcast, "Parents Are under Pressure—and We Can All Help," episode 56, September 4, 2024.
5. Blue Letter Bible, "Lexicon: Strong's G5412—*phortizō*," accessed February 19, 2025, https://www.blueletterbible.org/lexicon/g5412/niv/tr/0-1.
6. Johannes P. Louw and Eugene A. Nida, eds., *Greek-English Lexicon of the New Testament: Based on Semantic Domains*, vol. 1, 2nd ed. (New York: United Bible Societies, 1989), 53.

ONE | MORE THAN A MOM

1. Vicki Courtney, *Your Boy: Raising a Godly Son in an Ungodly World*, 2nd ed. (Nashville: B&H, 2012), 217.
2. Rachel Minkin and Juliana Menasce Horowitz, "Parenting in America Today," Pew Research Center, January 24, 2023, https://www.pewresearch.org/social-trends/2023/01/24/gender-and-parenting.
3. Timothy Keller, *Counterfeit Gods: The Empty Promises of Money, Sex, and Power, and the Only Hope That Matters* (New York: Penguin Books, 2016), xx.

4. Harold W. Hoehner, "Ephesians," in *The Bible Knowledge Commentary: An Exposition of the Scriptures*, ed. John F. Walvoord and Roy B. Zuck, New Testament (Wheaton, IL: Victor Books, 1983), 631.
5. Blue Letter Bible, "Lexicon: Strong's G4137—*plēroō*," accessed February 19, 2025, https://www.blueletterbible.org/lexicon/g4137/nlt/tr/0-1.
6. Barna Group, *Motherhood Today: The State of Moms and What It Means for the Church* (Ventura, CA: Barna and The MomCo, 2023), 9, https://www.barna.com/motherhood-today-free-digital-report.
7. Blue Letter Bible, "Lexicon: Strong's G4243—*presbeuō*," accessed February 19, 2025, https://www.blueletterbible.org/lexicon/g4243/niv/mgnt/0-1.
8. Jon Fogel (@wholeparent), "One day you'll miss the things that annoy you," Instagram reel and post, December 2, 2022, https://www.instagram.com/reel/ClrJTiPgjwd.
9. Timothy Keller with Kathy Keller, *The Meaning of Marriage: Facing the Complexities of Commitment with the Wisdom of God* (New York: Riverhead Books, 2013), 139.
10. Charlotte Huff, "More Couples Are Divorcing after Age 50 Than Ever Before. Psychologists Are Helping Them Navigate the Big Changes," *Monitor on Psychology*, November/December 2023, 58, https://www.apa.org/monitor/2023/11/navigating-late-in-life-divorce.

TWO | CANCEL THE GUILT TRIP

1. Reconstructed from memory of a real post from years ago.
2. Dictionary.com, s.v. "guilt (*n.*)," accessed January 7, 2025, https://www.dictionary.com/browse/guilt.
3. Kendra Cherry, "What Is a Guilt Complex?," Verywell Mind, updated December 5, 2023, https://www.verywellmind.com/guilt-complex-definition-symptoms-traits-causes-treatment-5115946.
4. Cherry, "What Is a Guilt Complex?"
5. Blue Letter Bible, "Lexicon: Strong's G2588—*kardia*," accessed February 19, 2025, https://www.blueletterbible.org/lexicon/g2588/niv/mgnt/0-1.

THREE | GOOD FOR HER, NOT FOR ME

1. "Social Comparison Theory," *Psychology Today*, accessed January 7, 2025, https://www.psychologytoday.com/us/basics/social-comparison-theory.
2. "Social Comparison Theory."
3. Dictionary.com, s.v. "ideal (*adj.*)," accessed January 7, 2025, https://www.dictionary.com/browse/ideal.
4. John B. Watson with Rosalie Rayner Watson, *Psychological Care of Infant and Child* (New York: Norton, 1928), 81–82.
5. Watson, *Psychological Care*, 84–85.

6. Anonymous, *Don'ts for Mothers* (1878; repr. New York: Cosimo Classics, 2014), 11–12.
7. *Don'ts for Mothers*, 4.
8. *Don'ts for Mothers*, 4.
9. *Don'ts for Mothers*, 16.
10. *Don'ts for Mothers*, 17.
11. Dictionary.com, s.v. "legalism (*n.*)," accessed February 19, 2025, https://www.dictionary.com/browse/legalism.

FOUR | SLOW DOWN AND SHOW UP

1. Vicki Courtney, *Rest Assured: A Recovery Plan for Weary Souls* (Nashville: W Publishing Group, 2015), 4–6.
2. Never Empty Nest by Melissa Neeb, "It comes too soon," Facebook, November 14, 2022, https://www.facebook.com/neveremptynest/posts/it-comes-too-soon/207244128366139.
3. Quoted in Zara Abrams, "How Can We Minimize Instagram's Harmful Effects?," *Monitor on Psychology*, March 2022, https://www.apa.org/monitor/2022/03/feature-minimize-instagram-effects.
4. Blue Letter Bible, "Lexicon: Strong's G4049—*perispaō*," accessed February 19, 2025, https://www.blueletterbible.org/lexicon/g4049/esv/mgnt/0-1.
5. Matthew Henry, *Matthew Henry's Commentary on the Whole Bible*, vol. 5 (Peabody, MA: Hendrickson, 1996), Luke 10:38-42.
6. Blue Letter Bible, "Lexicon: Strong's G4183—*polys*," accessed February 19, 2025, https://www.blueletterbible.org/lexicon/g4183/esv/mgnt/0-1.
7. Joseph S. Exell and Henry Donald Maurice Spence-Jones, eds., *The Complete Pulpit Commentary*, vol. 7, *Matthew to John* (Fort Collins, CO: Delmarva, 2013), Luke 10:42.
8. Henry, *Matthew Henry's Commentary*, Luke 10:38-42.
9. *I to Myself: An Annotated Selection from the Journal of Henry D. Thoreau*, ed. Jeffrey S. Cramer (New Haven, CT: Yale University Press, 2007), 201.
10. Henri J. M. Nouwen, *The Way of the Heart: Desert Spirituality and Contemporary Ministry* (San Francisco: HarperSanFrancisco, 1991), 25, 27.
11. Like the Legacy Standard Bible and the New American Standard Bible 1995.

FIVE | WORRY DOESN'T GET TO RUN THE SHOW

1. Caitlin Gibson, "Mothers Feel More Worried, Stressed and Judged Than Fathers, Pew Finds," *Washington Post*, January 24, 2023, https://www.washingtonpost.com/parenting/2023/01/24/mothers-stressed-worried-pew-survey. Other worries captured by the poll include children "getting beaten up or attacked, getting pregnant/getting someone pregnant as a teen, and getting in trouble with the police."

2. Gibson, "Mothers Feel More Worried."
3. Olivia B. Waxman, "Baby Jessica's Rescue from a Well Capped Off a Terrifying Week in U.S. History," *Time*, October 16, 2017, https://time.com/4980689/baby-jessica-30th-anniversary.
4. David Ropeik, "School Shootings Are Extraordinarily Rare. Why Is Fear of Them Driving Policy?," *Washington Post*, March 8, 2018, https://www.washingtonpost.com/outlook/school-shootings-are-extraordinarily-rare-why-is-fear-of-them-driving-policy/2018/03/08/f4ead9f2-2247-11e8-94da-ebf9d112159c_story.html.
5. "Child Mortality Rate (under Five Years Old) in the United States, from 1800 to 2020," Statista.com, January 2019, https://www.statista.com/statistics/1041693/united-states-all-time-child-mortality-rate.
6. Christopher Ingraham, "There's Never Been a Safer Time to Be a Kid in America," *Washington Post*, April 14, 2015, https://www.washingtonpost.com/news/wonk/wp/2015/04/14/theres-never-been-a-safer-time-to-be-a-kid-in-america.
7. "Fatality Facts 2022: Teenagers," IIHS, June 2024, https://www.iihs.org/topics/fatality-statistics/detail/teenagers.
8. Ingraham, "Never Been a Safer Time."
9. Ropeik, "School Shootings Are Extraordinarily Rare." As of 2018, when this article was published, approximately two hundred public-school students had been shot to death at school since 1999 out of about fifty million children who attend public school in the United States.

SIX | LESS STUFF, MORE MAGIC

1. Joshua Becker, "21 Surprising Statistics That Reveal How Much Stuff We Actually Own," Becoming Minimalist, accessed January 7, 2025, https://www.becomingminimalist.com/clutter-stats.
2. Christopher Willard, quoted in Shannon Lindquist, "Do Your Kids Have Too Many Toys?," Michigan State University Extension, November 20, 2017, https://www.canr.msu.edu/news/do_your_kids_have_too_many_toys.
3. See "Prenatal Education System, Plays Heartbeat Music in the Womb to Promote Bonding, and a Smart, Healthy Baby—Mom's Choice Award Winner, among Many Others!, White," Amazon, accessed March 23, 2025, https://www.amazon.com/BabyPlus-Prenatal-Education-Heartbeat-Promote/dp/B00140KS9I.
4. PB, Two-star review, "So far, is not living up to expectations," December 23, 2007, https://www.amazon.com/BabyPlus-Prenatal-Education-Heartbeat-Promote/product-reviews/B00140KS9I/ref=cm_cr_arp_d_viewopt_kywd?ie=UTF8&reviewerType=all_reviews&pageNumber=1&filterByKeyword=screaming.

5. Josh Sanburn, "America's Clutter Problem," *Time*, March 12, 2015, https://time.com/3741849/americas-clutter-problem.
6. Lindquist, "Do Your Kids Have Too Many Toys?"
7. Sanburn, "America's Clutter Problem."
8. Barbara Brody, "How Clutter Can Affect Your Health," WebMD, August 28, 2023, https://www.webmd.com/balance/ss/slideshow-clutter-affects-health.
9. Sanburn, "America's Clutter Problem."
10. Quoted in Sanburn, "America's Clutter Problem."

SEVEN | YOU MATTER TOO

1. Richard Swenson, *Margin: Restoring Emotional, Physical, Financial, and Time Reserves to Overloaded Lives*, rev. ed. (Colorado Springs: NavPress, 2004), 69.
2. Kendra Cherry, "What Is the Negativity Bias?," Verywell Mind, updated November 13, 2023, https://www.verywellmind.com/negative-bias-4589618.
3. Jocelyn Solis-Moreira, "How Long Does It Really Take to Form a Habit?," *Scientific American*, January 24, 2024, https://www.scientificamerican.com/article/how-long-does-it-really-take-to-form-a-habit.

APPENDIX | WHAT THE BIBLE SAYS ABOUT IDENTITY IN CHRIST

1. Adapted from Brittany Yesudasan, "Your Identity in Christ: How God Sees You," Cru, accessed January 24, 2025, https://www.cru.org/us/en/train-and-grow/spiritual-growth/core-christian-beliefs/identity-in-christ.html. Used with permission.

NavPress
Bold. Loving. Sensible.

Since 1975, NavPress, a business ministry of The Navigators, has been producing books, ministry resources, and *The Message* Bible to help people to know Christ, make Him known, and help others do the same.®

> "God doesn't want us to be shy with his gifts,
> but bold and loving and sensible."
> 2 Timothy 1:7, *The Message*

Learn more about NavPress:

Learn more about The Navigators:

Find NavPress on social media:

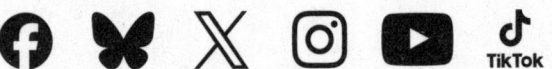